THE LAST CHILDREN OF MILL CREEK

D1280280

Enjoy!

THE LAST CHILDREN OF MILL CREEK

Vivian Gibson

Belt Publishing

Printed in the United States of America
First edition 2020

ISBN: 978-1-948742-64-1

Belt Publishing
3143 W. 33rd Street #6
Cleveland, Ohio 44109
www.beltpublishing.com

Book design by Meredith Pangrace
Cover by David Wilson

For my parents,

Frances Elizabeth Hamilton Ross

and

Randle Henry Ross

What she liked most was candy buttons, and books, and painted music … and the west sky, so altering, viewed from the steps of the back porch; and dandelions.

… But dandelions were what she chiefly saw. Yellow jewels for everyday, studding the patched green dress of her back yard. She liked their demure prettiness second to their everydayness; for in that latter quality she thought she saw a picture of herself, and it was comforting to find that what was common could be a flower.

—Gwendolyn Brooks, *Maud Martha* (1953)

Ross family, 1956, as printed in the *St. Louis Argus* with the caption "100% N.A.A.C.P. members. While Mrs. Ross spends numerous hours doing volunteer work in the N.A.A.C.P. office, the children are members of the junior youth and senior youth council."
Back row from left: LaVerne, Carol Jean, Shepperd, Randle, Beverly. Middle: Tootie, Randle H. Ross, Frances Ross. Front: Vivian and Ferman

INTRODUCTION

I did what Mama told me to do: "Move away so that I can have someplace to visit."

I moved to New York City in the summer of 1970. She visited me once in my third-floor walk-up in a brownstone on West 138th Street, between Broadway and Riverside Drive. At night, if I leaned against the right side of the window frame in my living room, I could look past Riverside Drive, over the West Side Highway, and down the Hudson River to the lights of the Jersey City waterfront. Or, I could look directly across the street through my neighbor's blinds that he never closed. But Mama seemed to enjoy just being in my space, among my things. She admired my secondhand furniture, much of which I had salvaged from posh Upper East Side curbs on bulk trash day. And she complimented the quality of the refinishing and reupholstering that I had spent several Saturdays working on before her visit. I had recently bought my first piece of new furniture: a chocolate brown Castro sleeper sofa that I slept on while she slept in my bed. It was the most money I had spent on any one item. During her weeklong stay, my favorite moment was walking up the stairs one day after work, hearing the television, and smelling chicken and dumplings—just like when I came home after school as a child.

My mother didn't get to see my favorite New York apartment (my fifth in six years). I sent her the new address in a letter describing the view from the French doors in my spacious living room. It was an iconic Morningside Heights city scene, overlooking the treetops of Morningside Park—the park that divided what comedian George Carlin called *white Harlem,* at the top of the sloping green space, from *black Harlem,* at the bottom of serpentine stone steps.

It was on the eastern edge of Columbia University at the highest point in Manhattan. In the distance, through a crowd of gray and brown apartment buildings with turret-like water towers on their roofs and fire escapes cascading down their sides, I could see the vertical marquee of the Apollo Theater on 125th Street. When Mama received my letter in St. Louis, she called me and said with a sigh, "Oh, I love the sound of your new address: 54 Morningside Drive. It sounds so prosperous."

———————

I was twenty-seven when my mother died in 1976. It was then that I realized how few in-depth conversations we'd had about *anything,* ever. By then, it was too late. My parents hardly ever talked about their lives before we were a family. I guess they were too busy working and raising eight children to ruminate on the past. And I was too busy thinking about myself to consider what was not shared. Besides, I thought we had plenty of time for talking—until we didn't.

I began writing family stories for my children before I had them. The loss of my mother, and, less than a year later, my father, created an urgency about preserving my memories for the children I would have someday. Children that my parents would never meet.

I remember a few stories from when Mama and her older sister would laugh and reminisce about their childhood in Alabama. She would answer any direct questions I'd ask about her childhood, but she rarely elaborated—as *Dragnet*'s Sergeant Friday would say: "Just the facts, ma'am." A college scrapbook found in the back of her closet yielded a bounty of pictures, notes, sorority memorabilia (she was a Delta), vacation postcards from friends, and even a postmarked envelope and note from my father that established when they met.

When I was in college, I read about the wave of African Americans who left the South by the thousands during the first Great Migration, between 1900 and 1940. My parents never mentioned it, but they were part of that exodus. They arrived in St. Louis eight years apart and under very different circumstances. Daddy came around 1929, with his mother and stepfather, from rural Arkansas so that he could attend high school. There was no high school for blacks near their town, and he was the first in his extended family to go beyond third grade. St. Louis was then a hostile city for black Americans: a former hub of the slave trade, with established customs, state laws, and zoning policies that mandated segregated schools and neighborhoods. Nonetheless, they considered their move a step up from the impoverished sharecropping life they'd left behind, just one state away "in the South."

Mama came eight years later. She was a pampered, middle-class college student from a small Alabama town where her father, a successful farmer, owned the "colored" grocery store. She came to St. Louis to visit relatives while on summer break. After my parents met that summer, and again at the next winter break, they soon married. My mother's life changed dramatically. They settled into a "Negro neighborhood" in downtown St. Louis called Mill Creek Valley and had eight children in rapid succession during the decade of the 1940s.

Mill Creek was one of the oldest parts of St. Louis. On land first developed by the Osage Nation, at the confluence of the Mississippi and Missouri rivers, it had been home to every new European immigrant group that arrived in the city over the previous one hundred years. As a French fur trading post at a bend in the Mississippi River, the central corridor grew westward, following the creek that powered one of the first grist mills in St.

Louis. The Mill Creek, as it became known, meandered from a spring near the current-day Chouteau and Vandeventer Avenues and emptied into the Mississippi River. Early citizens built grand homes near the shores of the creek; cattle grazed and watered at its edge. A dammed section became a man-made lake called Chouteau's Pond and was the site of the city's first public park (near where Busch Stadium is today). As the city grew, smoke-belching factories and foul-smelling slaughterhouses replaced the pastoral splendor along the bluffs of Mill Creek. Pollution and a cholera epidemic led to the draining of the creek in 1852. Railroad tracks that led to and from the bustling new central train station replaced the dried creek in the 1890s and established the southern boundary of the Mill Creek community.

The city's mostly white Anglo-Saxon Protestants pushed westward, building mansions along Lindell Boulevard and private, gated Vandeventer Place. The railroad tracks along the former creek bed provided a natural dividing line that eventually bisected St. Louis into north and south ethnic enclaves—Germans and Poles to the north, Irish and Italians to the south.

Eastern European Jews began immigrating to St. Louis in large numbers between1880 and 1920. Many lived in a Jewish "ghetto" they created along the near north side until, spreading westward from the riverfront as the city expanded, they moved beyond Jefferson, and then from Grand Avenue. Many in the Jewish community rented and sold homes they vacated on the north side to a burgeoning professional class of black citizens. Through the 1930s, '40s, and '50s, Jews moved to the central west end of the city, and to University City, north of Washington University, and Clayton in St. Louis County. Many continued to own the dilapidated tenements, substandard row houses, and Victorian-mansions-turned-rooming-houses they rented to migrating blacks in Mill Creek.

The Mill Creek neighborhood was bounded on the west

by Grand Avenue near St. Louis University, on the north by Lindell and Olive Streets, on the east by Twentieth Street, and by the railroad tracks on the South. Market Street was the main thoroughfare, lined with commercial buildings, small shops, theaters, dance halls, restaurants, and family-run businesses. The broad artery was punctuated at Compton and Market by Stars Park, one of only four Negro League baseball fields in the country, where the pennant-winning St. Louis Stars played their home games.

People's Finance Building was the bustling business center at Jefferson Avenue. East of Jefferson was a thriving entertainment district that ended at Twentieth Street with a sprawling train yard and the majestic white stone clock tower of Union Station. There were small pockets of well-maintained homes owned by black physicians, funeral directors, attorneys, and schoolteachers scattered throughout Mill Creek Valley. And churches abounded, ranging from magnificent cathedrals left behind by fleeing white congregations to modest "storefront" houses of worship.

In 1936 the City Planning Commission warned of the "central city abandonment" by European immigrants who increasingly identified themselves, if nominally, as "white" Americans and reinforced the racial divide in St. Louis. Newspaper editorials cautioned, "if adequate measures are not taken, the city is faced with gradual economic and social collapse."

"NEGRO INVASION" was the newspaper headline touted by local realtors, who gave homeowners notice that Negroes were encroaching on the all-white city neighborhoods south of Chouteau Avenue. Gail Melissa Grant, daughter of David M. Grant, a prominent Negro attorney and civil rights leader, wrote in her book *At the Elbow of My Elders* about her family's move across "the invisible dividing line" in 1947. Though attorney Grant was likely financially better off than his "largely blue-collar" white neighbors, "no amount of money or status could shield us from bigotry," his daughter wrote.

Considering the overt scare tactics used to control the migration of the city's black citizens amid renewed attempts to reclaim desirable downtown real estate, there was surprisingly little community protest. Guy Ruffin, president of the St. Louis branch of the NAACP and a teacher at Vashon High School, wrote a letter to the *St. Louis Post-Dispatch* in October 1948, in opposition to a proposed $16 million "slum clearance" bond issue. Ruffin claimed "lax enforcement of city ordinances" and city officials' "see-nothing, do-nothing attitude toward Negro neighborhoods" were the cause of widespread decay. Voters rejected spending money on the bond issue, but city leaders would try again a few years later.

My grandmother, Stella Hodges, was a domestic worker, the largest work category for Negro women identified in the *1947 St. Louis Urban League Annual Report*: it listed 2,308 cleaners in private homes, 656 laundry workers, 485 ironers, and 297 maids. Yet on December 16, 1950, my grandmother purchased a house from her landlords, Richard and Betty Bennett, at 2649 Bernard Street in Mill Creek for $1,400. She had saved the $100 down payment from her meager salary. Twenty years after leaving Earl, Arkansas, for St. Louis, she would finally have a home of her own with her son, his wife, and their eight children. She would be the last in a long line of owners of the hundred-year-old Italianate-style two-story dwelling.

My grandmother was unaware of the city's plans when she bought her house in the neighborhood where she had lived since leaving the South. However, politicians, realtors, and religious and business leaders knew what the future held for this 450-acre neighborhood. Egged on by a series of derisive articles in the local media, the city was moving to deem the area "blighted." The designation would pave the way for the eventual erasure of an entire African American community to make way for an interstate highway to the suburbs.

On August 7, 1954, less than four years after my grandmother bought her home, Mayor Raymond R. Tucker announced plans to relocate the residents of Mill Creek and demolish the "eyesore" in the heart of downtown St. Louis. He touted St. Louis as the home of "the nation's largest urban renewal project."

On May 26, 1955, the hardworking residents of Mill Creek Valley were going about their busy day. Most of them were unaware of what the headline of that day's *St. Louis Post-Dispatch,* about a bond issue passed by city and county voters, meant for their future. The looming and lasting change was buried in a list of twenty-three propositions that included hospital improvements, street widening, new parks, and new expressways. Listed merely as "slum clearance," the proposition allocated $10 million to acquire 2,000 homes, churches, schools, and businesses through condemnation or purchase, and demolish them for redevelopment.

The 1907 *City Plan for St. Louis* was one of the first comprehensive development city plans in the United States. The study focused on making St. Louis "cleaner and healthier" for its growing population, and a more "attractive city for visitors." The report proposed ambitious infrastructure improvements beginning with the "natural gateway" at the Mississippi riverfront. It included plans for open green spaces, European-inspired municipal buildings, and "modern homes" among the "undulating" hills spreading west, north, and south. There was little mention in that initial plan of the Negro residents that made up only 6.2 percent of the central city population at that time.

Aldermen passed a final measure on the Mill Creek plan on March 21, 1958, by a twenty-seven to one vote. The lone dissenter was Alderman Archie Blaine (Dem.), who initially supported the project. In the debate preceding the ballot, Blaine pointed out that "97 percent of Mill Creek is in my ward." He charged that no adequate provisions for rehousing the area's low-income residents were in place. "I'm in favor of better housing, but not in favor of slums moving to other parts of the city," he protested. The local League of Women Voters, the Archdiocese of St. Louis, and eventually, the NAACP endorsed the mostly federally funded project.

Eight months later, the first wrecking ball struck in Mill Creek and permanently destroyed a viable urban neighborhood of more than 20,000 people.

———————

This memoir is about survival, as told from the viewpoint of a watchful young girl—a collection of decidedly universal stories that chronicle the extraordinary lives of ordinary people. The tales recount rarely heard American history and culture through the family and community experiences that shaped the lives of the children living in a declining, segregated urban enclave. My father strived at multiple jobs as a truck driver, janitor, and church choir director to provide for his family. My mother, who created and sold handcrafted needlework, used her ceaseless ingenuity to lift her children above doggedly adverse circumstances. They tried to shield us from the painful realities of being what Toni Morrison called "Others."

They didn't talk about the perils of what lay beyond the invisible walls of our community. But they tried to arm us with what they thought we needed to survive: resourcefulness, a positive self-image, and an understanding of the value of hard work.

Millions who lived in mid-century American cities will find these stories of neighborhood streets, gangways, and alleys as playgrounds fondly familiar. Many others will read about a community with narrow choices that were stretched by sheer determination and enterprise—a visceral view of life across the tracks, or on the other side of town.

When I retired at age sixty-six, I started compiling stories I'd been writing for decades about the people I've known and loved. My first published story, "Hi Lizzie, I'm Your Mother," became part of a dramatic production—*50in50: Writing Women into Existence*, produced at the Billie Holiday Theatre in Brooklyn in 2017. My story "Sun Up to Sun Down" was published in Belt Publishing's *The St. Louis Anthology* in 2019.

In writing this book, I have indulged my passion for genealogy, history, and storytelling. I remembered and wrote about what I knew, or thought I knew, about a lost time and place in the hope of fostering better understanding of our present and concern for our future. I've travelled widely and lived, worked, and owned businesses in St. Louis, New York City, and West Africa. My enterprises were an extension of what I learned from my family as a child. After restructuring my hand-me-downs as the fifth girl, it was natural for me to design and merchandise women's fashions in New York and Liberia, West Africa. My early culinary adventures led to a catering business I called *Movable Feast* and the creation of a line of hot sauces aptly named VIB'S *Southern Heat* and VIB'S *Caribbean Heat*. A barbecue spice-rub straight from my daddy's recipe I called *BBQ Today,* reminiscent of a sign that hung on our front gate when Daddy sold sandwiches for church fundraisers.

I'm convinced that my zeal for living a full and authentic life is a direct result of my scrappy early years as one of the last children living and learning in Mill Creek Valley.

ONE

My mother grew up as privileged as a black girl in a small Alabama town could be. Her grandparents and great-grandparents had been enslaved there in Tuscaloosa County, and they remained there to sharecrop on the very same farms they had worked as Dempsey Williamson and Catherine Faucett's slaves. Generations later, my mother's family bore the evidence of the "open secret of the South"—people of mixed black and white ancestry, listed as mulatto in the US Census as late as 1920. No one openly discussed their origins. Mulattos lived among their black and white relatives like beautiful hybrid roses, with thorns no one dared to touch.

By the early 1900s, free from the yoke of sharecropping, Mama's father farmed his land and owned the colored store, euphemistically known as "The People's Store." His accomplishments made him a highly respected and well-positioned man in the community. He often served as a conduit between the black and white residents in Northport, Alabama, facilitating vital legal and business transactions. Whites purportedly designated such a person in every black community, in every Southern town, perpetuating the colorism that sustained a social order that divided the human race.

My mother was carefree, a bright and indulged youngest child in a family that had attained an elevated standing in their small riverport town. She enjoyed the love, hope, and attention that surrounded her. She had a charismatic personality, similar to her father's, that invited notice. But unlike her father, she didn't seek attention, she was just secure in attracting it. That was an unusual trait for a young black girl living in the first half of the twentieth century. Her demeanor and bearing made her appear comfortable with herself and everyone else.

Her name was Frances Elizabeth Hamilton, a lyrical, aristocratic name that suited her. The second syllable of Frances seemed to compel everyone to smile and then pause with expectation when they said her name. *Frances*. Can you imagine? Your name always ends with a smile.

She was taller than all the boys and girls in her classes. In a photograph taken at age eight, she was almost as tall as her sister Bennette, who was five years older. In the photo her long slender arms and hands hang relaxed, almost to the top of her knees. Slightly curved fingers guide eyes to her stretched, shapeless lower legs, then to proportionally angled feet that seem to prevent her long thin body from toppling forward.

An article clipped from the society page of a local newspaper in 1925 extolled the elegant occasion of her parents Ben and Della Hamilton's silver wedding anniversary celebration as "the crowning event of the present season." Her two older sisters were bridesmaids. "They carried pale pink roses and wore frocks of Georgette. Little Miss Frances, youngest child of the couple, served as flower girl."

She enjoyed a childhood filled with schoolwork, music lessons, and learning to crochet. A penchant for handicrafts led to hours of sewing, quilting, drawing, and her favorite, making flowers from crepe paper. Activities like feeding her pet raccoon on the veranda or chasing chickens in the backyard with cousins and neighbor children were always overseen by the watchful eyes of her mother.

Sundays in Northport were devoted to Porter St. Paul African Methodist Episcopal Church, where all the adults had titles that commanded a respect that was mostly absent in the broader community: Reverend, Mister, Miss, Usher, Deacon,

Trustee. Aunts and uncles were either blood relations or, more likely, trusted and longtime family friends. Family dinners of food raised on the Hamilton farm always followed church—fried chicken, peas, beans, tomatoes, carrots, sweet potatoes, corn, and okra.

Frances was the golden child of the five Hamilton children; a bit rebellious, athletic, outgoing, creative, and smart. Roles for females were evolving in the mid-1930s, just when Frances was headed off to college. Her brothers had taught her to drive their father's dusty Ford Coupe; she played guitar after rejecting the piano, which Bennette excelled at, and her height made her a natural basketball player. Soon, the controlled freedom of a college campus would open up a new world for her.

Frances and her parents likely boarded the train in Tuscaloosa in August of 1933, traveling sixty miles north to Birmingham and another fifty miles east through the lush foothills of the Blue Ridge Mountains to Talladega College. She had been to the campus the year before for Bennette's graduation. But it looked different this time—her time. They had gone scarcely a hundred miles from Northport, Alabama, where she knew everybody and everybody knew her. Now she was anonymous among the stately brick buildings.

Swayne Hall, the oldest building on the twenty-acre campus, sat at the end of the tree-lined main entryway. It was built with slave labor in 1853 as a boy's high school. After the Civil War, the Southern economy weakened, and the school, facing mortgage default, went up for sale. The former high school and surrounding acres were purchased with help from General Wager Swayne, director of the Freedman's Bureau, and funds donated by the American Missionary Association. A mere two years after former slaves had built a one-room schoolhouse for black children near the site, constructed with lumber salvaged from an abandoned carpenter's shop, the first private college for Negroes was established in Alabama. In 1867 a charter was struck for Talladega College.

Sixty-six years later on a hot August afternoon, families meandered along the paths lined with old oaks, tall pines, and sprawling magnolia trees that cut through the manicured lawns. As a child, in rare unguarded moments—usually when Bennette was around—I'd overhear snippets of stories about that first day on the Talladega campus. Mama remembered a flutter in her stomach, excitement, curiosity, and just a little bit of nervousness. She had never seen so many Negro people in one place. They looked unfamiliar, dressed differently, and talked in ways she had never heard.

Ben Hamilton strode proudly, ebullient in his self-appointed role as tour guide, his long arms waving in one direction, then another, as he pointed out the music building, the dining hall, and a newly built gymnasium completed since his last visit. Frances's thoughts drifted, wondering if she should have listened to her sister's advice about her choice of clothes to bring. Her mother, Della, scanned the day's itinerary and campus map, anxious to see the dormitory where her youngest daughter would be living during this next phase of her life.

Later that first day, at freshman orientation, Frances met her roommate, Eleanor Thompson, from a small town in Ohio. They spent the rest of the day together, whispering, giggling, and laughing about how the other talked.

Her soon-to-be friends, suitors, tablemates, and sorority sisters were the children of the black elite from all over the United States, Africa, and the Caribbean. They were future doctors, lawyers, educators, and business professionals of their communities. They were the very same young people that the celebrated educator and sociologist W. E. B. DuBois dubbed—in his famous debates with Booker T. Washington of Tuskegee Normal School—the "Talented Tenth."

DuBois wrote in 1903:

All men cannot go to college but some men must; every isolated group or nation must have its yeast, must have for the talented few, centers of training where men are not so mystified and befuddled by the hard and necessary toil of earning a living, as to have no aims higher than their bellies, and no God greater than Gold. This is true training, and thus, in the beginning, were the favored sons of the freedmen trained.

Frances wrote in her college scrapbook on Monday, October 22, 1934, her twentieth birthday: "Just another year older, but, oh what a difference just one year makes." How prophetic; she could not have imagined that by her next birthday she would be hiding a life-changing secret.

No one is alive today who witnessed the events of her life over the following three years. What I have been able to piece together comes from letters, documents, and family accounts, most of which are second- and third-hand. It was a familiar scenario that has played out in young lives countless times, as it still does today. She returned to college after the summer break in late August 1935, possibly unaware that she was two-and-a-half months pregnant. But by Thanksgiving break, the once rail-thin girl was noticeably fuller. There were stories that her father walked down Bridge Street in their hometown carrying a shotgun, looking for LJ Williams, a longtime neighbor and Frances's childhood friend, who had gone off to join the army by then.

On a blustery St. Patrick's Day in 1936, Gale Patrick Hamilton was born in Frances's home bedroom, delivered by a family friend, Dr. A. B. McKenzie, with the assistance of Frances's mother. The baby boy, named for that day's windy weather and the Irish holiday, was absorbed into their extended family. What decisions were made by a domineering father, a complaisant mother, and a daughter with promise who had shamed her family are unknown. Frances returned to college the following August, leaving the child in the care of her mother and her older sister, Mattie, who was married to a successful business owner and raising the first three of her five children.

In the summer of 1937, instead of going home to Northport for the summer break, Frances went for an extended stay with her mother's cousin and her family in St. Louis. The Days owned a neat two-family house at 2731 Spruce Street. Ethel Day was a schoolteacher, and her husband, Robert, was a chauffeur. Frances found a summer job as an elevator operator at a high-end downtown department store, known for hiring only attractive, light-skinned Negro women who eloquently announced the departments on each floor.

My mother met my father, Randle Henry Ross, that summer. He lived with his mother in a small second-floor apartment just a few blocks from where Frances was visiting her relatives. My parents enjoyed the summer together, and she returned to college in the fall of 1937. She visited St. Louis again for the Christmas break instead of going home, but barely three weeks later, on January 12, 1938, Frances's mother died unexpectedly.

Less than two years after starting college, Frances found her once-bucolic life unrecognizable. She did not return to Talladega. In a continued attempt to salvage Frances's reputation, her father's sister Eva took in baby Gale. Aunt Eva was in her mid-forties and had been married three times without children. She welcomed the child and doted on him.

About eight months later, on November 21, 1938, Frances married Randle Ross in his pastor's home, where Reverend William Munger lived with his family, above Northern Baptist Church at 514 South Ewing Avenue in the Mill Creek neighborhood of St. Louis.

In the 1940 census records, Gale Patrick, age four, was listed as the adopted child of Eva and her husband Jim

Edmonds; "Pat," as he was called, was given their last name. Also appearing in the US Census that same year was Frances, living in St. Louis at 2622 Bernard Street, in the Mill Creek community, with her husband Randle and their one-year-old daughter LaVern.

My parents' marriage cut across class lines. My mother had "married down." My grandfather did not approve.

My father was the grandson of Mississippi slaves, and the son of a thrice-married and divorced mother who had cleaned white peoples' homes and cared for their children in two states by the time they settled in St. Louis in 1929. They joined the wave of blacks moving north to escape the tyranny of Southern apartheid and seek a better education for their children. Arriving when he was fourteen, he attended the newly constructed Vashon High School—built to accommodate the city's fast-growing black community in Mill Creek.

By 1937, when he met my mother, my father was a truck driver who sang baritone in a quartet on weekends. He was handsome, with a deep, dark, smooth complexion punctuated with dimples when he smiled, revealing behind his full lips beautiful white teeth that shone like fine china. But nothing in his early years in the South, and little in the crowded, cold-water row houses in Mill Creek had prepared my father for my mother. She was a six-foot-tall and rail-thin college basketball star, whose milky-white complexion and shock of chestnut brown curls drew all eyes when she entered a room. Her subtle Alabama accent and mischievous smile embodied sophistication and breeding, the likes of which Daddy had never seen.

Mama's years as a wife and mother in St. Louis bore little resemblance to her early years, but her small-town Southern bearing was always perceptible beneath the surface of the urban poverty in which she found herself. She was different from most other women on Bernard Street. They had all travelled from Arkansas, Mississippi, and Alabama in that great black migration north during the 1920s and 30s. But to those who knew her before, it was surmised that Mama had left the better life behind.

She possessed a subtle self-confidence that came from a combination of training and appealing physical distinctions. Her college education afforded her a more refined manner of speaking, albeit with the upward gliding vowels of an Alabama drawl, and she charmed the Jewish store owners and insurance men who were the white people encountered most in our rundown enclave. "Hi, Miss Frances," is how the neighborhood children greeted her to elicit a warm "Hey, baby" in return.

Our neighbors were familiar with the broad range of shades among "colored people" from "light, bright, and damn-near white" to blue-black and every shade of brown in between. But white store clerks and waitresses assumed Mama was white when she glided up to the downtown department store counters of Stix, Baer & Fuller, or Scruggs, Vandervoort & Barney with her favorite hat angled just as she had seen in a recent issue of *McCall's* magazine.

During the early war years some items rationed to white women, like silk and nylon stockings that sold at inflated prices, were simply not sold to black women at all. Like so many coded rules of that time, women of color avoided the embarrassment of being told by an indignant white store clerk that the items they sought were "out of stock." So Mama enjoyed shopping for her friend Marguerite, who owned a beauty shop and was one of only a few black women she knew who could afford to purchase the highly prized hosiery. And while downtown shopping for her friend, she was always treated with the respect and service reserved for white customers when she sat and sipped a Coca-Cola at segregated lunch counters, just because she could.

On Sundays, she didn't attend the Baptist church with Daddy and many of our neighbors. She and her older sister Bennette (shortened to Bette), who had joined her in St. Louis in 1940, attended Jamison Memorial CME Church at the corner of Leffingwell and Washington. It was a historically black denomination of the Methodist Episcopal Church, like the one they had attended back home. The church would later change the CME in its name from Colored Methodist Episcopal to Christian Methodist Episcopal. She was the church secretary, and Aunt Bette was the Sunday School superintendent and played the piano for the children's choir. Aunt Bette, who had been a schoolteacher in Alabama, was now divorced, and had no children of her own, while Mama had two kids and another on the way by the time Aunt Bette arrived in St. Louis.

Aunt Bette and Mama were a matched pair of lithe alabaster beauties. Mama often laughingly encouraged her older sister, "C'mon Bette, let's go downtown and be white for the afternoon." They were mildly amused by their risky and fleeting forays into unwelcome territory. Their resentment of entrenched racism was assuaged only briefly by dressing up, boarding streetcars, and crossing the color line at will.

Daddy, meanwhile, looked like the man on the Cream of Wheat box: the iconic dark-skinned Negro with shining eyes and a wide grin showing faultless white teeth. His job was to maintain streetcar tracks and empty the trash at Public Service's bus garages and streetcar sheds throughout the city. He had a booming, perfectly pitched baritone laugh that came from his diaphragm deep inside his barrel chest. It was an honest laugh that we didn't get to hear until weekends and holidays, when he didn't work eighteen-hour days. The tone and timbre of his speaking voice made you forget the smell of gasoline and sweat on his gray work coveralls, and the thin orange sponge attached to elastic that stretched around his head to prevent the sweat on his forehead from dripping into his eyes. His careful diction deflected attention from the dingy, damp handkerchief tied around his neck. Daddy was of average height, about five foot ten, and round and robust—his big belly was hard, not jiggly, no doubt from lifting heavy trash cans and dumping their contents into the back of a truck for eight hours a day.

There was order and dignity in how my Daddy lived his life. That included laying down the law and enforcing it at home. Daddy didn't smoke, drink, or curse (except for the occasional "damn"). But the one infraction that would get us kids shocked out of a dead sleep by the crack of his long leather belt across the palm of his hide-like hand was leaving dirty dishes in the sink. The only child of a woman who was away from sunup to sundown taking care of the domestic needs of others, Daddy was left to cook, wash, and clean for himself as a child. So he had rules for cleaning the house, especially the kitchen. That was a good thing because Mama's indulged upbringing had not prepared her to be interested in nor proficient at any of those activities.

However, Mama did implement schedules and routines for chores. The four older girls rotated washing and drying dishes. My brothers Randle and Honey swept and mopped the kitchen floor, and I emptied the trash. Ferman, the baby, always seemed to be too young for any assignment.

Daddy would get home from his second job as the janitor at Northern Baptist Church around 10:00 p.m.—enough time to eat something, watch the late evening news, and go to bed for the night. All the children were in bed, asleep or at least pretending to be, when Daddy passed through the middle room to the kitchen each night.

The need to keep trash and garbage out of Daddy's sight was understood by all. His cardinal rule was: "Eat everything you put on your plate." If he happened to see uneaten rutabagas, half-eaten cornbread or, God forbid, meat left on a chicken or pork chop bone in the kitchen garbage after dinner, he hit the ceiling. "Who threw this good food away? Y'all can throw away more with a spoon than I can bring in with a shovel."

If you were awake when he got home, you would have to do something that was not one of your assigned responsibilities, and there was no greater indignity than to be told to wash a dish left in the sink when it was not your day to wash dishes. But the worst infraction was when Daddy felt a greasy plate or glass because somebody washed the dishes in cold water.

The single light bulb hanging from the ceiling would flash on with a snap of its dirty, waxy string to reveal wide-eyed children cowering in their beds. Daddy would bellow, "Get up, get up, get in that kitchen and clean it." Some brave soul would whimper, "Daddy, it's not my day."

Daddy's answer was always the same: "I don't care whose day it is, all of you get in there and clean that damn kitchen."

Mumbled accusations flew as we shuffled around the crowded kitchen in mismatched pajamas, threadbare nightgowns, and oversized undershirts. We heated water for dishwashing, re-swept, and re-wiped until we heard the reassuring sound of Daddy's snoring coming from the front room. Only then did we peel off in silent resentment and return to our beds. He would be up again in six hours to go to his day job.

Needless to say, we didn't see Daddy much. If you avoided the magic dinner hour during the week, and were in bed by ten o'clock at night, you could go without seeing him until Saturday morning. He left home at five o'clock in the morning. When he arrived back home at precisely five o'clock in the evening, he had forty-five minutes to eat his dinner from a folding TV tray while watching the evening news. This strict ritual took place in front of our two used and stacked televisions—one with a picture and no sound, the other with sound and no picture.

At 5:45 p.m. he then walked two blocks west on Bernard Street to Ewing Avenue and another half-block south to Northern Baptist Church. He had lived in no less than six locations in a four-square block area of this neighborhood for the past thirty years. Every man, woman, and child knew who he was and could set their clocks by his trek. As he passed, there were familiar refrains: "Evening, Ross." "Hi, Mr. Ross." Maybe even "Hey, Daddy." Other greetings were simple nods or a slight wave of a hand.

Our church was one of the scores of former churches and synagogues left behind as the white congregations moved west with the expanding city and county. Daddy unlocked the church for the evening services and meetings, then proceeded to open windows in summer and adjust the furnace in winter. He cleaned and made minor repairs until 10:00 p.m. on most nights. On Tuesdays, he interrupted his cleaning to conduct choir rehearsals. On Wednesday nights he tiptoed in and out of prayer meetings. And on Thursday evenings he joined the male chorus rehearsals. The weekly practices and the choir members who attended them made up a large part of Daddy's social life. You could feel the air of camaraderie and frivolity, mixed with pride in their musicality. Even the laughter before, during, and after rehearsals vibrated on pitch in the otherwise empty sanctuary. Singing was a simple joy that he managed to squeeze into his crowded life.

Our way of living was greatly influenced by how Daddy lived as a child in Earle, Arkansas, which was honed from his mother's experiences in turn-of-the-century Mississippi. She had lost a child in a fire as a young woman and had to leave Daddy alone before and after school while she worked. We heard the familiar Southern father's story about having a hard life growing up in "the country." Daddy "chopped wood in the morning, then walked five miles to school with no shoes." Sometimes the story was embellished to add "in the snow." We got no sympathy from him when we were stuffing cardboard in our shoes to make them last to the end of the school year. And he would get mad if he saw us playing outside in "perfectly good shoes" in the summertime instead of going barefoot. But it worked for me—I loved the feel of warm dirt sifting through my toes. It was like he had picked up Earle and plopped it down in the middle of St. Louis. And of course Daddy's nothing-wasted attitude was most important when it came to food. Not that we had any leftovers—my brothers made sure we ate everything at every meal. But Daddy could find comfort food in the dregs of a meal—more commonly known as *pot liquor.*

Pot liquor is the flavorful and nutritious broth left over from a pot of greens. It's a rich liquid seasoned with smoked pork, salt, pepper, vinegar, and the tangy, tart flavor of slow-cooked turnip, mustard, or collard greens. It could be used as a tonic for a sick child or a hearty base for soups or stews. But Daddy drank it steaming from a bowl like a soothing hot toddy after coming in at night from his second job.

Sometimes there were one or two slices of cornbread left over as well, wrapped in waxed paper and set to the side for Daddy to crumble into his pot liquor or his other catch-all liquid, buttermilk. He and my grandmother could munch on buttermilk-soaked cornbread like it was a bowl of ice cream. With sugar sprinkled on top, it's not half bad.

Though pot liquor, buttermilk, and cornbread were not uncommon among Southerners, Daddy also enjoyed other, more enigmatic edibles—he loved to gnaw on bones. He was okay with others throwing bones away once all the meat was eaten from them. But he enjoyed bone marrow, and he went for it—chicken bones, pork chop bones, even neck bones that were gnarly and hard, he gave them his best shot. When he was finished with a neck bone, it was gray and dry like a carcass that had been baked in the desert sun. But the pièces de résistance were pork rib bones that were the rack for meat he had smoked and basted with vinegar-water for six hours in our backyard on the Fourth of July. The combination of time, low temperature, and moisture rendered the collagen in the bones to a pliable density that he chewed and savored long after others had moved on to dessert.

Finally, there were two staples that accompanied every meal except breakfast: a whole (as in unsliced) peeled yellow onion, that he bit into like an apple, and a jar of cold water, kept in the refrigerator at all times in a designated sixty-four-ounce Sho-is-Fine syrup jar with a top—known exclusively as "Daddy's water." No one was allowed to drink it so that it was always cold and available whenever he wanted it.

TWO

"Mama raised us from her bed."

I don't know if Randle was being critical of our mother or praising her, but I too have a vivid recollection of Mama sitting on her bed, partially reclining with two pillows tucked snugly against the small of her back. After Daddy vacated his side at sunrise, Mama would smooth the sheets and blankets, spread a muslin "drop cloth," and replace him with a tan, boxy leather suitcase she pulled from beneath the bed. A piece of furniture for sleep and rest became her workspace for the remainder of the day and sometimes late into the evening. Mama left this space periodically throughout the day to wash clothes and prepare meals or supervise Ferman and me as we played nearby.

The suitcase both served as a hard work surface and stored the tools and materials she needed to be productive. Its contents changed depending on her project, but usually included straight pins, tape measures, various sizes and shapes of needles, spools of crochet and sewing thread, large scissors for cutting fabric, small scissors for clipping and trimming, and pinking shears for edging. There were yards of neatly folded fabrics, rolls of ribbons, and stacks of precision-cut shapes for quilting. Pattern books and pictures clipped from magazines and newspapers were pinched together with spring-clamp clothespins. There was always a pencil and a 5 x 8 inch pad of paper with notes, lists, sketches, and partially written letters that eventually got mailed to friends and family members who lived in other cities.

Next to her bed was a small table with a telephone and a lamp that my brother Randle had made in his eighth-grade wood shop. The wooden base of the unshaded lamp had two upright dividers that provided space to store bills to be paid, other mail, and Mama's dog-eared phone book. Teetering on the edge of the table was a cup of tepid tea that she sipped from throughout the day. The delicate teacup was one of two from the Country Roses collection that she bought when they caught her eye at a secondhand shop on Market Street. The one she used almost every day had a small chip on the base. The other sat on the top shelf in the kitchen cabinet next to the pressed-glass fruit bowl we never used.

She would often position herself on the edge of the bed, with one of her long pale legs over the side, resting her bare foot gently on the floor. Her heel raised, the ball of her foot and toes were poised as if ready to sprint at a moment's notice. Our two stacked televisions were just feet from the foot of her bed. She turned them both on soon after the older children left for school. The steady stream of toothpaste and detergent jingles, game show hosts cheering on contestants, *The Charlotte Peters Show* at noon, and afternoon soap operas provided background noise that was incongruent with the beauty her nimble fingers created. Their smooth, repetitive, unceasing motion engendered a calm focus when she tugged at the soft cotton thread from a spool hidden in the folds of her bedcovers and crafted the simple string into the patterned fabric that would soon grace someone else's table, chair, or bed.

A casual observer might see a languid, cluttered scene. Nothing was further from the truth—her displays of creative ingenuity provided a significant supplement to the income my father brought in from his three jobs. Mama was a prolific and sought-after producer of handmade home decor and fashion accessories; her intricate tablecloths and bedspreads adorned the homes of our neighbors, church members, friends, and friends of friends. As more women worked outside their homes, my mother was a one-woman holdout in a fading cottage industry. Crocheting and quilting was a tradition that many women had abandoned when they left the South, but Mama took it to another level—she crocheted skirts, vests, hats, purses, even dresses.

She took afternoon and evening craft classes at the YMCA, community centers, and hobby shops, sometimes attending weeklong courses in leather crafting, jewelry making, or plaster mold casting. Each new skill necessitated new tools and materials. St. Louis was prominent in the millinery supply and hat manufacturing industries, and she took classes offered by the millinery supply companies along Washington Avenue and Locust Street.

We lived in 800 square feet: three rooms on the first floor of my grandmother's house, filled mostly with beds. There was no room for a worktable, there wasn't even room for any chairs. So from her bed she crafted leather handbags and wallets from unborn calfskin, and pieced hand-cut pieces of tanned hide together with thin strips of leather lacing. Using metal stamps and wooden mallets, she embossed the leather with initials and motifs. She traced images from magazines or pattern books onto thin sheets of polished copper or tin— using specialized tools and a mallet to hammer relief portraits of human profiles or Chinese pagodas into the sheets of metal. Then she rubbed shoe polish into the recessed areas to highlight the designs, framed them, and sold them as wall hangings. By the time school was out each afternoon and children began to fill our small house with noise and activity, the foot of her bed displayed some sort of finished craft that we took for granted and barely noticed.

By far, her most successful creations were her millinery designs. She sold fancy ladies hats as fast as she could make them. The weeks before Easter each year, Mama's bed looked like a plush garden of pastel blooms growing from molded straw and airy netting. In the fall, her bed appeared to be crowded with brown, gray, and black exotic nesting birds displaying colorful and iridescent plumes.

I tagged along as Mama and my sisters fanned out on Saturday afternoons, delivering tissue-paper-wrapped parcels to homes and beauty salons, and were greeted with squeals of joy and frenetic searches for the nearest mirrors. Occasionally, Mama and I would end our deliveries at the Barcelona Tavern, where we visited with Mama's friend, Miss Cora, who opened the bar, replenished the inventory, and set up before the Saturday night crowd arrived. I liked everything about being inside of the Barcelona—the twang of the blues that kept a beat with the rotating colored lights coming from the jukebox, and the reflection of the glasses and bottles that sparkled in the mirror behind the bar. I loved smelling the sweet smoke that permeated the air, and spinning around on the barstools. My cheeks caved in when I sucked ginger ale through a straw to get to the cherry at the bottom of the glass. Sometimes Mama was delivering a parcel to Miss Cora, but more often the delivery was for one of the bar patrons who would come in later in the evening. Miss Cora would collect payment and pass it on to Mama later in the week.

My favorite of Mama's creations were the beautifully realistic flower corsages she made for Mother's Day. From 4 x 4 inch sheets of man-made flock material that had the look and velvety feel of rose petals, she would cut hundreds of irregular tear-drop shapes. She assembled artificial flowers, petal by petal, by coiling a single thin wire to hold each petal and leaf in place, then covered the wire with green paper tape to give the appearance of a stem. The finished arrangements of rosebuds and full blooms were made into ribboned corsages and boutonnieres to honor mothers. On Mother's Day we children were her dedicated salesforce—selling her creations on the street corner where my brother Honey sold Sunday newspapers and outside our neighborhood churches. We punched holes in cardboard box tops to carry and display our wares. We offered red flowers to churchgoers with living mothers and white flowers for those whose mothers had passed away.

Like everything she crafted, the corsages sold quickly. Before rushing off to Sunday school, we ran back home and dropped the money from our sales onto Mama's bed. She would be dressed by then and ready for church—changed from her cotton housedress into a tasteful gabardine suit that accentuated her waist and a wide-brimmed hat that balanced her height. Her hat would be trimmed with grosgrain ribbon and silk flowers or an artfully angled feather that she'd likely finished just before going to bed the night before.

Mama always took a taxi to church on Sunday mornings and intentionally timed it so she arrived just as opening prayers were beginning. As church secretary, she stood to the side of the pulpit to read the morning announcements, some of which were hurriedly handed to her as she entered the church. When the weekly reminders and expressions of appreciation were read, she then walked down the long aisle to sit near the rear of the sanctuary where she could admire her handiwork as worn by many of the stylish worshipers. After the benediction, it was not unusual for women to rush over and ask if the hat she was wearing was for sale. It was.

―――――――――

I liked my mother. She made everything seem effortless. She was easy to be around and had a pleasant manner that made everybody comfortable in her presence. Liking my mother made loving her easy. I could sit with her on the wooden bench just inside our front gate and be quiet as she talked to neighbors who stopped to chat as they passed. I'd lie across the foot of her bed that always had the faint smell of the Cashmere Bouquet perfumed talc that we gave her for Christmas. She rarely looked up from whatever she was crafting, but she would always answer, explain, console, or cajole in the same even, confident tone that left me feeling rewarded. If I sensed her disappointment, I was wounded, and I fear I disappointed as much as I pleased.

In addition to being pretty, friendly, and fun, Mama was the smartest person in my world. Reading while sitting on the floor, propped against her bed, I'd start to spell a word aloud that I couldn't decode: "A-T-M-O-S—," and she would calmly say, "atmosphere." I was amazed. I'd read on, hoping for another word beyond my ability for the excitement of again witnessing the magic of her pulling the word right out of the air. She would answer any question I asked as if she were my personal encyclopedia—and I had lots of questions.

Most everybody liked Mama, except for two women: One was Miss Ester, the daughter-in-law of Mr. Glassman, the Jewish man who owned and operated the store where we did our trading. Ester and her husband, Howie, the owner's son, lived upstairs over the store during the week. Daddy worked for the Glassmans on Saturdays, stocking shelves and boxing and delivering groceries when he and Mama were first married.

Mama came to the store on Garrison Street, near the Mill Creek railroad tracks, every Saturday morning to cash Daddy's paycheck, shop, and settle our account. We made purchases "on the book" during the week when Mama would send us to the store for incidentals. Mama used her church-secretary-reading-the-Sunday-announcements voice when requesting to see the accounts journal. At six feet, she looked down on the grim-faced store clerk, and when she adjusted her shoulders backward, she gained another essential inch. Miss Ester glared and never spoke a word while Mama carefully checked the entries and totals before paying something on what was owed. Howie Glassman, in contrast to his wife, always yelled a gleeful greeting over the meat counter when Mama walked over to select two chickens for Sunday dinner and whatever bony, fatty meats she needed to stretch our weekly meals.

Daddy and my brothers picked up and delivered our groceries on Saturday afternoons after they finished working at the church that was just one block over from the grocery store. There was always laughter between my parents about what Miss Ester had to say when my mother wasn't around. Mama's "arrogance" was more than Miss Ester could handle. But the coolness that emanated from Miss Ester didn't bother Mama one bit.

The other woman who did not like my mother was my grandmother, my father's mother, who lived in the rooms above us. There were few words wasted between my mother and her mother-in-law even though we all lived in the same house for years. They were skilled at avoiding each other. It was easy—Mama just had to be in her bedroom at 5:00 a.m. when Grandmama came downstairs to leave for work, and in the kitchen at 5:00 p.m when Grandmama trudged up the stairs after work. I never heard a harsh word or a raised voice between them, but I never saw a smile either. We children were the go-betweens and messengers. Grandmama was referred to by my mother as Miss Hodges—tell Miss Hodges this, take Miss Hodges that. Daddy was the fulcrum on which both women rested—central to their coexistence and function in our household. My grandmother did my father's laundry weekly and made his lunch every day. I'm sure my mother gladly acquiesced; she had plenty of washing and cooking to do already.

My grandmother joined many of the women on Bernard Street who left home before daylight to catch as many as three streetcars that transported them to manicured communities just west of the city limits. They arrived early to homes where they cooked and served scrambled eggs for breakfast and readied white children for school. The rest of their day was spent cooking, cleaning, and doing laundry until boarding streetcars in the evening that returned them home just in time to go to bed. Grandmama said that there were sundown laws that mandated people of color to be off the streets in the county by sunset. If she had to work late, her "white folks" (that's how she referred to her employers) would drive her to the Wellston Loop to catch an eastbound streetcar back into the city.

My grandmother was in bed for the night by 7:30, which was our time to be quiet. A slammed front door, a burst of laughter, or the rhythmic thumps of Sam Cooke singing "Another Saturday night and I ain't got nobody" on the radio would elicit familiar rapping on her bedroom floor. There was a broomstick leaning against the wall—an arm's length from her bed—just for the purpose of pounding a signal for silence. Sometimes, out of frustration, she would shuffle in her well-worn slippers to the top of the stairs and call down to my mother, in a commanding tone made no less threatening by her shaky, weary voice: "Frances, make those children be quiet." It usually worked for the rest of the evening.

Halfway up the stairs that led to Grandmama's rooms was my favorite retreat from the constant hum made by the ten people inhabiting the three small rooms below. The worn wooden risers and treads of the steps created a perfect work desk for cutting out Betsy McCall paper dolls. The eagerly anticipated monthly issue of *McCall's* magazine provided me with hours of cutting out brightly colored paper dresses, coats, and hats that I carefully crimped onto Betsy's posed body. More hours were spent drawing new outfits of my own design. Using the smooth white cardboard that formed Daddy's freshly laundered Sunday shirts into a starched folded rectangle, I cut and crafted small easels that held my paper dolls erect for miniature fashion shows.

That space that divided Grandmama's quiet from our constant hum held another appeal for me—it was an opportunity to eavesdrop on my grandmother's cloistered existence just feet away. There was always a low murmur from the brown molded-plastic Zenith radio that sat on the crowded table just inside her bedroom door. The black rotary telephone that took up most of the remaining space on the small table rarely rang in the evening. But when it did, I leaned in and pressed the side of my face against the upright wooden balusters and positioned an ear to hear what was said. Sometimes I could tell it was one of the sisters from the church, usually Mother Vine. Mother Vine was a feisty and friendly old lady who always smiled and stroked my face on Sunday mornings when we arrived at the church. She tilted my chin upward and looked me in my eyes in a way that my grandmother never did. She would always ask, "How's yo' mama?" as if to distract me while she magically presented a peppermint candy from her purse. I couldn't see Grandmama's face, but I could hear a slight smile in her voice after she said, "Hey, Vine." Their phone conversations never lasted long and ended with a wry, knowing chuckle followed by, "You get some rest now, bye."

Other times when the phone rang, I would hear a voice and words that I hardly recognized. Her side of the phone conversation started with the usual questioning "Hello?" Then changed to an unfamiliar subservient "Yes, ma'am." After a pause her voice changed again to a soothing maternal tone that I only heard during these exchanges, "I know," she'd say reassuringly. "You be a good boy now. Go to bed, and I'll be there when you wake up in the morning."

There were eight children in our family. The oldest was LaVerne, who went by "Vern." Her first name was Henry—

which was my father's middle name. She later spelled Henry with an "i" at the end and occasionally pronounced it with her version of a French accent. Randle was next, and the oldest boy. His first name was Edgar after my father's father. That's all we knew about my paternal grandfather—Randle had his name. Beverly came next, willful and stubborn, bossy and moody. She looked the most like our grandmother—but, boy did she hate hearing that, so of course we mentioned it every chance we got. Carol Jean was number four. She was the pretty one (which was Beverly's *real* issue), tall and fairer than the rest. Teenage boys called her "high yella" in awkward attempts at flirting. She had long, thick hair and a reluctant smile. We called her Jean, and she was "all business," like Mama. Shepperd, named after our pastor, Felix Shepperd, at Northern Baptist Church, was nicknamed "Honey." He was shy, industrious, and agreeable. Tootie's birth name was Thelma, but nobody called her that. Even her teachers called her Tootie after the second day of school. She had a permanent smile on her face and soft cottony hair that she wore in three short braids that turned up at the ends like commas. There is a three-and-a-half year gap between Tootie and me. I'm not sure how my siblings would describe me. But I remember that I was constantly fighting for my share of attention. My name, Vivian, is from my mother's childhood neighbor who everyone called "Aunt Vib" (with a b). Vivian Nalls played the piano for silent movies in their hometown theater in the 1920s. I never met her, but she sent me a silver dollar every time Mama returned from a trip to Alabama.

The baby boy was Ferman Drew, eighteen months younger than me. He was cute and smart. I was often reminded that he learned just about everything before I did—including *almost* spelling *my* name. Everyone thought it was so adorable when he gleefully rattled off "Vi-vi-vi."

Frenetic morning activity ended abruptly in our house when the last of the big kids slammed the front door and went off to school. The slap of wood and whoosh of air whirled dust into the streak of sunlight straining against the single dirty window in the middle room.

The hour before was a hubbub of purposeful commotion, lots of individual activity, not a lot of talking. Everybody knew what they had to do and the time allotted to accomplish it—a well-rehearsed morning routine. Ferman and I sat up in our bottom bunk like spectators with front row seats to our family theater. We were not allowed to talk to the players and not allowed onto the crowded stage.

Tootie—eight years old with Daddy's round face and smiling, full lips—needed help lifting the pot of water from the front burner of the kitchen stove. She wanted to pour the steaming water into the galvanized face-pan placed on the white enamel-topped kitchen table by herself. Jean, three years older than Tootie, interceded, grabbing a terry cloth dish towel singed at the edges from its frequent encounters with the open flames of the stove. Using the dish towel to hold the hot pot handle, Jean poured heated water into the shallow face-pan. She was careful to use only half, leaving some hot water in the pot for Beverly. Jean filled a waiting Mason jar with water from the kitchen faucet and added it to cool the steaming water enough for the two younger pigtailed girls to wash their faces and hands. Giggling, they shuttled a huge, slippery cake of Ivory soap between them.

Across the small table, Honey stared, hypnotized, into a large mixing bowl half filled with cornflakes, canned evaporated milk diluted with water, and sugar. Hunched over the bowl, he robotically spooned cereal into his mouth, then lifted the bowl to drain it with loud slurps to get the last drop of the watery milk. He may or may not have made use of the water left by his sisters to splash his face and hands after breakfast. And he may or may not have used the dish towel to dry his face and hands. Honey quickly dressed and performed his morning chores: dragging trash cans to or from the alley and picking up the backyard debris left from the previous day's after-school playing.

Beverly poured the remaining hot water into the same hastily rinsed face-pan and snarled at how little hot water was left for her to use. She closed the kitchen door for privacy and quickly washed before one of the boys would burst through the door, asking for his lunch. Beverly then methodically laid out two rows, four slices each, of Wonder Bread on the table and spread each slice with a messy smear of Miracle Whip sandwich spread. She carefully unwrapped two heavy bundles of brown butcher's paper, slipped off the red rings of plastic casing from the thick slices of baloney, placed a slice of the garlicky, pink meat on each slice of bread, followed by a slice of American cheese, and topped it with a second slice of bread. She neatly wrapped one sandwich for herself in waxed paper and left the kitchen. Everyone else had to wrap their own sandwiches: one each for the girls, two for Honey, and three for Randle.

Randle would eat one of his sandwiches while walking across the Jefferson Bridge to Attucks Elementary. His morning routine, like the diagonal scar through his right eyebrow, fed into his tough-guy self-image. He brought in wood and coal to fuel the potbelly stove in the middle room, shoveled snow from the front steps when needed, and emptied and reset the basement rat traps. He always asked if Mama needed something from Mr. St. Clair's store across the street before he left for school. She always did. Mama, half reclining, waiting for the house to clear of children, gestured with a slight uplift of her chin and told him to take a precise amount of money from the purse at the foot of her bed. He raced across the street and hurried back with a dollar's worth of pork neck bones, or a loaf of bread, or two onions. He never brought back change, and Mama never asked—hoping to prevent Randle from taking some poor kid's lunch money to buy himself a few loose cigarettes.

Vern moved upstairs to live with Grandmama when the long-time boarder, Miss Etta, vacated the small front room on the second floor, joining Grandmama's exclusive club as the only two people in our family to each have a room and a bed to themselves. At fourteen, Vern became a shadowy figure who lofted through the front door and up the stairs with her eyes straight ahead. She descended the stairs each morning with a simple "bye, Mama" as she left to join her friends to walk in the opposite direction of her siblings to Vashon High School, the same high school Daddy had arrived in St. Louis to attend nearly thirty years before.

Just about every city-dwelling child of the 1950s has a tale about having to be home when the streetlights came on. When daylight began to wane, children of all ages knew where they were supposed to be. They drifted homeward, as if pulled by invisible apron strings, to avoid the ultimate embarrassment of having their mothers come to look for them. My rowdy brood of sisters and brothers was no exception.

Winter or summer—no matter the weather, we stayed outside as long as we could. When the streetlights came on, Ferman and I had to go inside. The older kids had to be in front of the house, usually huddled around the light so that Mama could see them from the front window. My older brother Randle was routinely missing. Mama would eventually exit the rickety screened door and plant her feet on the paintless planks of the side porch like an Amazon warrior in a cotton print housedress. Her natural beauty was accentuated by an ever-present errant curl that she brushed back with a single sweeping motion of her hand, circling upward then around to come to rest at her mouth. With her thin lips pulled back tightly against her teeth, her thumb and middle finger expertly curved to almost touching between her slightly parted lips, Mama took in a deep breath through her nose and forced air from her lungs, over her tongue, and through her teeth and fingers to make a piercing whistle: a two-part, birdlike shriek that skidded on the night air and carried to the middle of our city block. Only then did Randle coolly stroll to the waiting glow of the streetlight. He hung back just out of sight every night so that his friends could hear and be in awe of his mother's unrivaled summons.

Daddy was rarely home in the evening when the molded concrete lampposts topped with frosted glass orbs glowed softly to usher in the close of day. But occasionally he would whistle too. His sound was louder and more menacing than Mama's. We didn't hear his signal often, but it had a distinctive whoosh and snapped like the crack of a whip. He deftly tucked in his bottom lip and forced out a long breathy screech followed by a rapid staccato of pop, pop, popping air. All the running, jumping, and wrestling kids in the neighborhood stopped in their tracks—eyes wide, heads cocked to one side, and necks craned like a herd of deer in listening poses. They all recognized his salient call. Searching out Ross siblings in various groups of playing children, someone could be heard saying, "Yo' daddy's home." Even Randle would breathe a hushed "ah shit," his mind racing to remember what chore Daddy might had found undone. When we heard Daddy's whistle, we instinctively knew what it meant: everybody come home, right now, and you're probably in trouble. If we were lucky, his whistle simply meant he wanted us close to home—on the front sidewalk or in the backyard.

The backyard just before dark is where we could always see The Cat—that's what we called the mottled gray muscular tabby that roamed the perimeter of the cold-water, two-family dwelling. It strode, brushing against the fences between the yards and the back alley, a predator methodically patrolling its territory. I always knew it was there, but I didn't look directly at it. We never thought of that cat as a family pet. It was utilitarian, practical, like a farm animal. Its purpose was to control the rats. We didn't name it or touch it; we didn't feed it. Mama must have given it water and scraps during the day, which accounts for its loyalty to our house. All we wanted was for The Cat to hunt rats at night.

But in late fall and winter, the rats came inside at night. Daddy and the boys plugged holes with steel wool held in place with chicken wire and hammered flattened tin cans in corners where the floor and baseboards met. Huge powerful rat traps had permanent positions in the stone-walled basement where my brothers slept in summer.

On a brisk November evening, my brother Honey and I were sitting on the back steps, waiting for the last light of day to fade before we had to go inside for the night. The Cat slowly emerged from behind the coal shed at the far end of the backyard and paused—as if to indicate it was her yard now. Honey glanced up and, rising from the step, confessed to an unasked query: "I'm more afraid of the cats than the rats—especially at night when they sound like babies crying in the alley." I was reassured to hear it was cats I heard at night and not babies. As if egged on by The Cat's appearance, we entered our dimly lit kitchen and closed the door behind us.

I slept every night with my clunky brown school shoes held snug against my chest. Other six-year-old girls might have been snuggled up with a rosy-cheeked doll or the soft pile of a well-loved teddy bear. Not me. I didn't even like dolls and teddy bears. My shoes were my security against the threat of the mostly unseen, nighttime rats that scurried across our floor or gnawed at something from within the walls next to my bed.

Everybody had their nighttime maneuvers for dealing with the rats. The older girls used the toilet before going to bed and didn't have to get up during the night. That didn't work for me. Mama said I had a small bladder. In a moderately successful attempt to curtail my bed-wetting, I'd hold tight to my trusted shoes just in case I had to get up to go to the toilet in the dark. With all the courage I could muster, I'd throw a shoe as hard as I could into the middle of the floor and wait for the rats to retreat deeper into the walls. My brother Honey, who coached me on my nocturnal plan of action, slept with his trusty stick and could occasionally be heard striking a sharp blow to the floorboards.

Sometimes at night, when all was finally quiet, there would be abrupt, but familiar skirmishes, followed by a cacophony of screeching and squeaks, scratching claws, thumps, and thuds. At first, I sucked in a sharp breath and stiffened, then raised my head slightly to hear with both ears. My eyes opened wide against the darkness of the middle room, where I slept in one of the four bunk beds. Ferman slept peacefully at the opposite end. Staring into the night, I didn't want to see anything. My wide-open eyes just made me more alert—I listened with my whole body. After a long, tense minute of quiet, I could hear The Cat crunching on the bones of a dead rat. A calm washed over me—I relaxed. I was safe. The Cat had done its job.

When I made it through the night without being eaten by a rat or The Cat, I went outside with everybody else to play as soon as I could and for the entire day. As much as I enjoyed playing house and school, drawing outfits for paper dolls, and cooking (both pretend and real), those were pretty passive endeavors. I liked what my brothers got to do: hit, throw, swing, climb, bang, and chop. When you're almost four years younger than your next sister and eleven years younger than the oldest girl, you hear a lot of nos, not nows, and—the most hurtful—get-out-of-heres. Beverly and Tootie were fast runners and could beat most any boy in a foot race in their bare feet on hot asphalt. Beverly really liked boys and equated outrunning them with flirting. Tootie jumped double-dutch all day, all summer. I couldn't do it. She and her friends didn't want to take the time to teach me. Besides, I couldn't master the rhythm needed to time, step into, and skip over two ropes whirling alternately in opposite directions. Jean kept her fingernails long and polished, and would not do any activity to jeopardize them. Like Mama, though, she could whistle expertly, using her thumb and middle finger. Jean was pretty, everyone said so; boys really liked her and weren't interested in whistling competitions. Vern only liked girls' stuff, books, and being left alone.

I wanted to climb trees and fences and jump off the roof of the coal shed into a pile of leaves with the boys. I was determined to throw a baseball—"not like a girl." I spent hours practicing my boxing "bob and weave." Randle said I had "good form" when I tucked my chin and held my fists high to protect my face—"for when I got into a fight."

One Christmas my little brother got a football. I got a brown rubber baby doll with painted-on hair and eyes that shut when it was laid down. It came with a bottle that I filled with water. Seconds after squeezing water through a hole in its mouth, the water trickled out of a hole in the doll's rounded bottom. My interest in that peeing doll lasted about five minutes. I wanted Ferman's football because I also had "good form" when I took the football back, then forward, right past my ear. My hands were too small to grip the ball very well, but I got it to go straight for a short distance.

Randle and Honey were always building things. I'd watch as they leaned in toward each other, their heads almost touching. They talked sparingly, but intently, as they worked together—lifting, sawing, positioning, holding, and hammering. I may have been a little jealous; I was definitely curious. When Randle would leave, I'd ask Honey to let me nail or saw something, and he would show me what Randle had just taught him. After a few instructions, I was able to make the perimeter walls of my playhouse more structurally sound with the addition of a few rusty nails I found lying around.

In summer the boys built skateboards out of two-by-fours and the wheels from metal roller skates. They labored over race cars made from wooden milk crates, outfitted with baby buggy wheels mounted on a piece of wood that pivoted on a single nail when tugged by a rope tied to each end. And every fall, what was usually considered work became play.

As the season started to change, trucks would appear in the streets of Mill Creek piled high with firewood and mounds of black, dusty coal for sale. Most people bought their wood and coal from the trucks each week—but not us. We never knew where Daddy got anything, but one day in late September we'd come home from school, and there would be a sprawling pile of freshly cross-cut logs in our yard. My brothers and their friends made games and competitions of splitting the large circumferences of tree trunks into pieces small enough to fit into the stove that heated our house.

Randle had been chopping wood the longest, so of course, he was in charge. He fell into his familiar role, barking orders and making rules. First thing was to find a piece of wood that would serve as a chopping block—a large section that would be the surface on which to place logs for splitting. The chopping block had to be the right height off the ground—which was a few inches below Randle's knees—making it easier to swing and land the ax without bending too low and hurting your back. To get started, he used a sledgehammer to pound the ax head as a wedge into the large sections of green wood. He knew how to "read the grains" in the wood and how to avoid the knots, to control the size of the pieces of wood chopped.

Splitting wood was dangerous play for these boys; a glancing blow of the ax could send wood ricocheting in unpredictable directions. I think that was one of the competitions—who could send a piece of wood flying off the farthest.

On the outside watching, I wanted to learn how to swing that ax, even though it was almost as long as I was tall. As usual, the key for me entering the realm of boydom was to wait for Randle to leave and ask for Honey's help. We started with a hatchet and small pieces of wood that had already been split. Standing the wood upright, I learned to find the spot where I wanted to chop, rest the hatchet on that spot, set my feet apart directly in front, aim, and swing. After a few misses and near-misses, I tried to do with the hatchet what the older boys did with the ax. I held the hatchet with my left hand at the end of the handle, and my other hand below the head of the hatchet. I lifted the iron blade straight up over my head, sliding my right hand down until both hands met at the end of the handle; with outstretched arms and unblinking eyes, I lowered the heavy wedge and hit my spot. By the end of that day, I was chopping kindling for starting fires.

Years later, when I was about a foot taller than that beckoning ax, I learned to choke up on the smooth curve of the handle the same way I did a baseball bat. I'd flex my knees, shift my weight slightly while raising that most basic of tools up, over my head, and down in one sweeping motion to split logs like a boy.

Every school day morning, on cue, with the final slam of the front door, Mama magically appeared at the middle-room door. The dusty atmosphere was different—quieter, slower. Mama hummed as she made oatmeal or Cream of Wheat for Ferman and me. Sometimes she made her favorite—warmed leftover rice with butter, sugar, and bits of crumbled bacon sprinkled on top. She insisted that the day-old rice absorbed the flavor of the butter and sweetness of the sugar better than freshly cooked rice.

My mother's hands were never idle. She was in the kitchen cooking daily, or washing clothes in her washing machine with a clothes wringer on top. The wringer pivoted in place over the tub so that water from the wet clothes drained back into the washer. There was a predictable loud popping sound that came from the kitchen when she overloaded the wringer cylinders and forced them apart in a sudden violent release. When she wasn't in the kitchen, she was in the front room, paying bills, writing letters, and doing her handwork on the bed that served as her workspace.

At those times, just feet away from Mama, I was in charge of playing. On cold or rainy days, Ferman and I played in the small square hall where the three rooms of our home converged. When we played house, he pretended to be the baby and would lie obediently on a folded quilt pallet. He even made baby sounds and gestures that he perfected when my mother picked him up and bounced him in her arms, as she asked adoringly, "Who's my baby?" He'd draw his arms up beneath his chin and bounce them so that his limp hands flopped up and down, emitting an unintelligible whimpering sound that somehow pleased my mother. When we played school, I placed him on the bottom step that led to my grandmother's rooms upstairs. I'd teach him his ABCs—as my sister Jean taught me. I'm pretty sure he learned them quicker than I did—which only made him more adorable.

When he got tired of me, or I of him, I'd spend hours playing alone in our extended backyard, a space made narrow by my grandmother's vegetable garden, which stretched behind a sturdy, wooden, fortress-like fence built by my father and brothers. The rest of the yard was all dusty grayish-brown dirt—not a blade of grass in sight. But the dirt, trod down by the feet of playing children to a fine flour-like texture, was perfect for mud pies. And I was serious about making my mud pies with that delightful dirt. I used a piece of discarded window screen to sift out tiny pebbles, chips of wood, and shards of glass. In the hollow of a dug-out hole in the ground, I mixed in water and stirred with a small stick to achieve the desired consistency. Imitating Daddy's Sunday morning biscuit-making routine, I'd pat out a double handful of mud onto the carefully dusted bottom step that led to Grandmama's back porch. With a lid from a Mason jar, I cut out precise circles of the silky-smooth mud, then carefully moved my moist mud pies to the second step, which was my pretend oven. While they baked in the sun, I sometimes picked the poisonous deep-purple berries from the poke salad plant that grew wild on the side of the coal shed, and added them to the top of the dried pies. I admired my culinary clay for a while, showed them off to Mama to get an approving smile, then diligently started all over again.

Around age six, I progressed from making mud pies to peanut butter and jelly, and then baloney and cheese sandwiches, and from tuna salad to deviled eggs. Learning to cook was a significant milestone in my development and was reflected in my eagerness to impress my parents. "Now you're cooking with gas," Mama would say with approval. She was not a gusher; when you overcame your challenge, no matter how small, and were successful, her metered smile was the equivalent of a knowing wink, as if she was patiently waiting for the inevitable.

Cooking bolstered my sense of accomplishment and gave me the confidence to explore new and sometimes dangerous activities. Living and playing around a red-hot stove that sat surrounded by beds taught me to respect and live with fire at a young age. Using heat and flame to cook was a natural progression for me. But kneeling down and reaching underneath an oven to light a gas pilot with a flaming piece of twisted newspaper led to a sharp learning curve. One of many unsupervised incidents resulted in a whoosh of flames that singed my eyelashes and eyebrows. Undaunted, I quickly learned the required timing for turning on the flow of gas and the application of fire to hissing holes in the metal pipes beneath the oven.

One morning when I was not quite tall enough to stir a pot of sputtering oatmeal, my shirt sleeve caught the handle. Before I knew it, the pot tipped and dumped the hot oatmeal all over my lower legs and feet. My bobby socks alone protected me from serious burns—another lesson learned. Though admonished to not use the stove without supervision, I persisted and had only one other serious episode: my frayed flannel shirt sleeve caught fire this time. I ran the short distance from the kitchen through the middle room screaming, "FIRE!" Mama met me as she rose from her perch on the side of her bed, grabbed the collar at the nape of my neck, and yanked off the burning shirt in one sweeping motion. While she examined my arm, I noticed the curtains behind her were burning. Unflappable, she turned, stretched her long, once-athletic body across the bed, yanked down the flimsy fabric, threw it to the floor, and stamped out the fire. Slowly turning back to me and wagging her head in resignation, she warned, "Girl, one day you're going to burn us out of house and home."

Determined, by age eight I had learned to cook fluffy rice and cobblers with flaky pie crust, and I soon perfected the essential: cornbread. I knew my cornbread was good when Beverly commanded me, without the slightest hint of sisterly praise, "Make some cornbread for dinner."

My oldest sister, Vern, had taught me how to make the golden-brown disk of goodness using only sight and my hands for measuring. I learned to confidently combine three heaping handfuls of yellow cornmeal and one heaping handful of flour, half a cupped palm of salt, a full cupped palm of sugar and the same of baking powder, two eggs, and enough buttermilk to thoroughly moisten all the dry ingredients. Vern was careful to remind me to add the buttermilk in small amounts until the batter was just loose enough to pour, but not runny. She repeated an important rule that Miss Savannah, her godmother, had told her: "You can always add more milk, but you can't take it out."

I patiently waited for the temperature of the hot iron skillet to transfer to the rendered bacon grease that generously covered the bottom of the blackened pan. Mixing half the flavorful hot fat with the barely fluid consistency in the mixing bowl, I then quickly poured my concoction into the skillet. The sizzling edges of batter that spread along the bottom and up the sides of the hot cast iron formed an immediate perfect crust that filled me with pride. (It was the same secret pride of accomplishment that I felt the day I realized the word *yesterday* was the first three-syllable word I spelled correctly in the Friday spelling test.) Then I waited, as the heat of the oven evaporated the moisture inward and away from the surface of the bread, and the crust rose slightly into a crispy ring of crunch. I'd know it was ready when a shallow crack in the center of the bread formed as the last steamy moisture escaped like a dying volcano.

When I placed a big wedge of my creation on Daddy's plate and announced, "I made the cornbread," Mama smiled. Daddy would take a big bite and proclaim: "My baby sho' can cook."

Pleasing my parents was always my reward, but when they were not pleased, there was a predictable punishment—a whooping. "Whooping" is likely one of the first words that black people garnered from the language of slave traders throughout the African diaspora—a variant pronunciation of the whip used to control their human chattel. Or maybe it was derived from the sound the flogging instrument made when it cut through the air. The harsh tradition of corporal punishment was firmly ingrained in the ethical values of Christian European enslavers. Sadly, that legacy of brutality carried on in the culture of many black Americans, who saw few options for controlling their children. When Daddy, our teachers, some neighbors, even pastors in church whooped our asses, they said it was for our own good, that they were trying to keep us on the straight-and-narrow path to safety in an unfair and intolerant society.

Our whoopings had an added dimension of terror that we called the "whooping line." It started with Daddy ordering his children in a chilling, calm tone: "Git in here and line up." Waiting in the line for your turn was worse than the first strike of Daddy's thick leather belt. If you closed your eyes and braced yourself, you got two or three stinging swipes across your butt, and it was over. Daddy kept an accounting of our infractions in his head. He could have noticed a growing buildup of dust under the beds or around the perimeter of the floor because someone swung broad sweeps with the broom, scattering dust from the middle of the floor. Or he found unwashed pots hidden in the oven. And there was always a note from school about poor performance or bad behavior to be addressed. These terrifying episodes usually occurred on Friday or Saturday evenings, and were deterrents for most of us. But Beverly and Randle saw things differently: if they were going to get whooped anyway, they figured they might as well do something to deserve it. Beverly was always "acting grown," and often not where she was supposed to be, while Randle was smoking, getting into minor skirmishes, and basically being a "lovable thug."

I've been told that by the time I was old enough to graduate from Mama's threats of spankings, which never happened, to joining the rear of the whooping line, the frequency of the whoopings had slowed. However, I do remember lining up according to age. Vern's big eyes that looked most like Daddy's squinted and squeezed out tears as she whimpered like a puppy. Randle took his whoopings bravely, mostly because he had done or not done more than the rest to cause the lineups. The girls all cried long before they were hit—except for Beverly. She scowled and stared defiantly at Daddy and refused to cry. Randle may have gotten the hardest licks, but Beverly may have gotten the most, because she absorbed them with a stubbornness that made Daddy angry.

Jean was next and cried the loudest; she hopped and twisted and flailed as he held her by one arm. She pleaded and called on the name of "Jesus" to stop Daddy before he even raised the belt. Eventually, he got three strikes in and let her go. Honey stood just out of Daddy's reach and immediately started to negotiate. "Daddy, I didn't mop the kitchen floor last Tuesday because you told me to go to the church after school and empty all the waste cans. By the time I got back home, ate dinner, and did my homework, it was time to go to bed." Daddy didn't want to whoop Honey; Honey was his dependable "road dog" who Daddy relied on to get chores done right. So he gave him three respectable boy-swats and let him go. Tootie had been weeping and patiently waiting for her two taps; he gave them to her then moved on.

Meanwhile, I used my time at the end of the line to stuff toilet tissue in my underwear or put on a second pair of pants. Unlike Tootie, I yelped and darted toward Daddy, grabbing his legs. I ran around him like he was a Maypole. He twisted and turned, hitting himself as he tried to hit me. By that time everybody's tears had turned to sniggers; he was tired and let me go. I don't remember baby Ferman ever being in the whooping line.

When a lot of children live in a small space like ours, lining up is second nature. In addition to lining up for corporal punishment, we lined up with bowls in our hands to be filled with beans, spaghetti, or sauerkraut and pig tails at dinner time. There was always somebody or -bodies squirming outside the toilet door yelling, "Hurry up." And on special occasions there was even a line for Mama to take our pictures.

The photographs from our childhood rarely included an image of Mama because she was usually running toward us with her Brownie camera—the one with the big round flash attached to the side—yelling, "Wait! Wait! Let me take a picture." Posing for pictures on our way to church on Easter, school dances, and graduations were Ross family rites of passage.

In one of the dozens of Sunday morning pictures, I'm wearing my favorite sky-blue sailor dress. We always took our pictures in front of Mr. Trotter's brick-and-stone fence next door. It looked so much better than our tattered board fence and gate that was built by my brothers with scraps of wood we stored behind the coal shed.

In many of the pictures, we squinted our eyes and tilted our heads down to avoid the sun shining in our eyes, because Mama said, "Shadows should be behind you for the best light." In those pictures, it's easy to notice that our hair was not our best feature. The parts in our hair were always crooked or off-center. As creative as my mother was, she could not manage to tame her young daughters' manes. Sometimes when we arrived at the church on Sundays, church ladies would take us downstairs and re-comb our hair. I think Mama pretended not to notice when we returned home from church looking better than when we left.

Once a year, on a Saturday before Easter, Mama had our hair straightened with a hot metal comb heated over an open flame by Daddy's cousin, Brownie. She was called Brownie because of her reddish-brown complexion, and we kids dropped the the "s" in the word "cousin" to call our family beautician Cou'in Brownie.

Even when our hair was straightened, Mama still braided one side tighter than the other, giving it a lopsided appearance. Even worse were all the other weeks of the year when we didn't get the kinks and tangles oiled and pulled through that smoking-hot iron comb to straighten it to twice its previous coiled length. During those other fifty-one weeks of the year, our hair was relentlessly puffed-up and frizzy around the edges of our hairline, the ancestral European genes powerless against the dominant genes of our African ancestors. So vexing was that new growth of undulating hair, it evolved into its own one-word insult: "edges." The only derogatory reference worse than edges referred to the similarly unruly curls of hair at the nape of the neck, called "the kitchen." Every female in church on Sunday (and Lamont, the junior choir director) could relate to the popular saying regarding hair "along the edges and in the kitchen" of their hairlines: "fried, dyed, and laid to the side."

Mama's soft brown curls bore the DNA of her anonymous Caucasian progenitors. Consequently, she had no experience with nor the dexterity to part, tug, and smooth our resistant hair into neatly woven braids. As in so many other aspects of our young lives, my mother enabled us to be resourceful and self-sufficient, learning to groom our own and each other's hair very early in childhood.

However, in honor of Jesus rising on the third day, we rose early on the Saturday before Easter to get our hair done. Cou'in Brownie lived on Jefferson Avenue near Market Street. Her house abutted the busy sidewalk and had no front yard. The front door sat back under a tall arch of red brick at the top of four steep steps. The bottom half of the door was painted wood panels, so passersby could not look inside. The top portion had an etched frosted-glass window. If you squinted, you could see through the etched design down the narrow hall clear to the back door.

We arrived early, five sisters with our hair washed the night before, parted and braided into six wooly sections. The door was unlocked, and we entered yelling down the hall, "We're here Cou'in Brownie." She yelled, "Come on back, Vern, I'm ready to take you first." And so our long day of waiting began as she fit us in—in order of age—between customers who paid the five dollar price to have their hair pressed and curled in her kitchen-salon. Because we were family, we spent only one dollar each "to get our hair done."

Saturdays at Cou'in Brownie's were always adventures. My sister Beverly, sulking, stared out of the window onto Jefferson while waiting her turn. Tootie and Jean chattered and giggled as they leafed through the captioned pictures of black celebrities in *Ebony* and *Jet* magazines. I was all ears while the women rotating in and out of Cou'in Brownie's kitchen talked about everything and everybody in the neighborhood. If we were still there into the afternoon, we would buy a fifty-cent box of pork and rice from the Chinese takeout spot across the street and share it while sitting on the back steps. But if we were lucky, we got to hear Cou'in Brownie pray.

Many of the full-price customers were members of her church and called her "Sister Wooten." After their curls and waves were made to shine like patent leather, and before they handed over a five dollar bill, Cou'in Brownie "laid hands" on their shoulders, necks, arms, or legs with a vice-like grip and began a loud, forceful beseeching of God to heal whatever ailed or troubled them. With her head thrown back, she ended the spellbinding prayer with deep guttural sounds from her throat that seemed to cough any pain, stiffness, or sorrow right out of the sufferers' jerking bodies.

My newly straightened hair aside, those extraordinary visions of exorcism were worth every hour I spent in waiting.

In Mill Creek, every aspect of life was labor intensive and time consuming. We boiled water to wash dishes, clothes, and our bodies; we built fires to heat the house, and walked everywhere we wanted to go. On the rare occasion we rode a streetcar, it was never just a straight trip—we always transferred at least once, maybe twice to get to our destination.

But we turned every chore into a game, a competition, or a lesson. Before we had a steam iron, clothes and sheets that needed pressing were sprinkled with water, rolled tightly, and placed in the refrigerator to be kept moist until ironing commenced. Retrieving the damp, tightly tucked laundry from the fridge was the beginning of the ritual. It was performed in exactly the same way every time and carefully taught by one sister to the next in a domestic rite of passage. First, roughly dried cotton garments were plucked from the outdoor clothesline in spring, summer, and fall. In winter, or on rainy days, collapsible wooden racks were set up in the kitchen. There was also an indoor clothesline that hung on the back of the kitchen door, coiled like a cowboy's lasso. It was suspended across the room and tied to a metal hook secured to the doorframe on the opposite side. Some days, freshly laundered clothes were dried on chair backs, and sheets draped from one bedposts to another. Mama washed clothes every day, and the first thing we did when we got home from school was take the laundry down and fold them before ironing. The space behind the potbelly stove was reserved for socks and favorite sweaters and blouses we washed by hand for school the next day.

Everything we wore was made of natural fibers, primarily cotton in summer and wool in winter. Nobody could be seen at school or church in wrinkled or poorly ironed clothes, so the iron and ironing board were as essential as a washing machine and dresser drawers. Our ironing board stood behind the kitchen door, never far away because it was used every day but Sunday. Not ironing on Sundays was one of Daddy's strict, unquestioned, and presumably Bible-based rules—like eating fish on Fridays, even though we weren't Catholic. Our iron didn't have a temperature control and, as with a lot of appliances in our house, the control knobs were broken or missing. So the implement was either on or off, and either hot or burning hot. Therefore, great care and attention were required to avoid scorching a beloved blouse that had been handed down from one Ross sister to the next. All the girls ironed their own clothes, and Mama designated someone to iron Sunday shirts for the boys. Daddy's one indulgence was to send his Sunday shirts out to the laundry.

The jockeying and squabbling for who got to iron first started on Friday evenings, picked up again early on Saturday mornings, and went on throughout the day. The ironing was squeezed in between cleaning (both house and church), high school football games, swim meets, shopping, part-time jobs, sock hops, and what Mama called "courting." Never far from earshot, that involved LaVerne, Beverly, and Jean sitting at the front gate or on the front steps under Mama's window, talking to boys.

On such evenings, Daddy, taking his cue from the announcer's nightly question on the television—"It's 10:00 p.m. Do you know where your children are?"—would make his way to the front door. The teenagers sensed his presence even before they heard the sweep of the screen door across the stone step. His terse baritone command was meant to strike fear in the boys: "C'mon in the house—the rest of y'all go on home."

His words scattered the couplings as the boys mumbled, "Yes, sir," over their shoulders as they retreated, and my sisters ducked under Daddy's arm as he held the screen door open. With all the Ross kids in the house, Daddy turned the skeleton key to lock the door for the night and returned to his room. Beverly almost immediately went to the window in the middle room, climbed out, and continued her visit with Bull Lattimore. Bull, as he had many times before, cut through the gangway, jumped over our back fence, and was waiting at the side of our house like a cool Romeo waiting for his naughty Juliet to descend.

The almost perpetual ironing ritual would begin anew by dissolving dry Argo starch in warm water and carefully pouring the starch solution into a large Vess soda water bottle. The bottle top had several holes poked in it with an icepick for sprinkling. The crimped edges of the thin tin top made it easy to pinch the edges for a tight fit. The holes in the bottle top were easily covered with your thumb, as constant shaking and remixing of the starch was required throughout the ironing process. Off to the side, table salt was sprinkled onto a doubled sheet of waxed paper to make an abrasive surface for cleaning the inevitable build-up of starch from the surface of the iron.

I was taught the "right way" to iron a blouse or shirt. First, sprinkle a moderate amount of starch onto the already damp collar and firmly apply the hot iron in constant motion, back and forth until the steam stops and there is a pearl-like sheen. Next come the sleeves, then the shoulders and the back yoke. The back bodice follows, and the front bodice is last. We used the correct names of the garment parts because we knew them from regularly thumbing through Mama's pattern books.

There was a different and more tedious kind of ironing that Mama did mostly when we were at school. The cotton doily designs she spent hours crocheting had several feet of ruffles that had to be starched and ironed dry until they stood up like petticoats for tabletops. The starch for stiffening the billowing ruffles was made by boiling equal parts of white sugar and water until the sugar completely dissolved, but before it crystalized. When cooled, she dipped damp doilies in the liquid starch until thoroughly saturated, then squeezed out the excess. After covering the ironing board with a clean white cotton pillowcase for further absorption, she painstakingly ironed the limp gathers inch by inch until dry. Working quickly, she shaped the ruffles while they were still warm into symmetrical looping waves that soon cooled and hardened until they stood inches high like delicate white filigree. The standing frills surrounded a flat center on which table lamps would be placed. Every fall some of the doilies reappeared for washing and ironing, but Mama never entrusted their care to us.

As the youngest girl, I enjoyed learning to do the things my mother and sisters did, and ironing was no exception. They were happy to pass on the responsibility of maintaining my clothing to me. I took pride in learning to use the dangerously hot iron to transform wrinkled, shapeless pieces of cotton clothing into crisp, smooth, lustrous apparel. After a few minor mishaps of scorched fabric, which were easily concealed by sweaters or by keeping the offending char turned away from prying eyes, I became an enthusiastic, if not competent, ironer. I'd hang my freshly pressed garments on the bed railing and admire them all Saturday afternoon and evening until I donned them for church on Sunday mornings. Mama alone acknowledged my handiwork with, "Don't you look pretty?"

On Saturday mornings, all of the Ross children dusted pews, emptied trashcans, swept and mopped vestibules, or shoveled snow and salted the steps of the church.

But Saturday nights were relegated to getting ready for long Sundays at church. We shined our shoes, ironed our dresses and shirts, and laid out our clean underwear. The older girls curled their hair and secured the curls with pink foam rollers. When the rollers ran out, they resorted to torn strips of brown paper bags twisted, then tied around their coiled hair, Buckwheat-style. Then we took our Saturday night baths. Every middle room or kitchen in our neighborhood was warmed with steaming pots and kettles of boiling water that filled galvanized number three washtubs. It was a routine that started early in the evening with the older girls first. The radio was tuned to the black station, KATZ 1600 AM, with the smooth voices of disc jockeys like Spider Burks and Lou "Fatha" Thimes introducing each song and reading commercials with the same cool patter. My sisters scurried to form a spontaneous stroll line. Side by side, they cross-stepped, bobbed, swayed, waved their arms, snapped their fingers, and sang along loudly to the sweet falsetto of Little Anthony and the Imperials singing "It Hurts So Bad."

Pouring and splashing from the tub mingled with the R&B coming from the radio, and the swaying continued as the hot iron glided across Tootie's white blouse with the Peter Pan collar that Jean wore the year before as a junior usher at church. The indispensable brown craft-paper bags—torn and flattened—served as barriers to prevent shining and scorching while ironing the box pleats on navy-blue Sunday skirts. It was the only time the middle-room door, hung with a rack of heavy winter coats, was ever shoved closed. Honey and Randle had to stay outside, where they shined and lined up all the Sunday shoes while watching *Gunsmoke* on the televisions with Daddy until the girls were done. Ferman and I bathed next and splashed until the lukewarm water we shared was cold. Then, Randle and Honey carried the tub to empty it outside the back door. They closed the kitchen door, refilled the tub, and in Mama's description, "Threw water up in the air and ran out from under it."

When the bathing, ironing, and shoe shining were done, we popped popcorn in bacon grease, made red Kool-Aid in two half-gallon jars, and waited for the boys to tell scary stories. They set the mood by turning off the lights; in winter there was just the orange glow from the potbelly stove. We sat in a circle on the floor while Randle loomed over us from his perch on the side of one of the bunk beds. He told the stories in his practiced scary cadence. Honey would ease away from the group—we pretended to not notice. At a prearranged point in the story, Honey pounced in the middle of the floor with his high-pitched version of a roar, and we all scattered, yelped, and screamed until Grandmama pounded on her floor above. We all hushed at once and stifled our laughs with puffed cheeks and hunched shoulders. That was our cue to finally go to bed.

Sunday mornings began with the smell of Daddy's homemade buttermilk biscuits: large baking pans full of browned mounds with fluffy white centers. We'd slather them with that good government-issued butter, drench them in Sho-is-Fine syrup, and eat them with thick slices of crispy, smoked jowl bacon. Then we all quickly dressed and walked the few blocks to the church, following behind Daddy like eight baby chicks. Grandmama came to church later with a lunch she packed specially for Daddy, because Sunday was just another long workday for him.

It was Mama's habit to stay out of the intense morning activity until the house was cleared. She attended Jamison Memorial, the Christian Methodist Episcopal Church, along with Aunt Bette's family, her husband, Uncle Skeets who also sang in a quartet with Daddy, and our cousin Karen.

When Jean became a teenager, she decided to go to church with Mama, and Tootie soon followed. They didn't have to attend Sunday school at Jamison Memorial, so along with Mama, they became the de facto Sunday cooks. As soon as the dishes were cleaned from breakfast, they fried chicken, made onion gravy, boiled and mashed potatoes, and baked cornbread. Any desserts, greens, or beans that took longer preparation were cooked on Saturday nights between the ironing and bathing.

Sundays were full days for us, too. We were the first to climb the broad steps that led to the elevated main entrance to the church. As Daddy's oversized bunch of keys jangled while he unlocked the door, he barked out last-minute cleaning assignments like a drill sergeant. I got to dust the throne-like chairs and lectern in the raised pulpit as church members started drifting in. Then we attended Sunday school, sang in the various choirs, and served as junior ushers. For me, there was the special treat of friends that we only saw on Sunday because they lived a few blocks on the other side of the church and attended different schools.

But the best part of going to church for Randle—and what kept him showing up like clockwork—was second offering. The first money collection involved the congregation leaving the pews and lining up to place their money in a basket on a table in the front of the sanctuary. The second offering was for special fundraising projects and came later in the service, after the choir sang but before the sermon. The baskets were passed along the seated worshipers at chest level. Every Sunday, Randle placed his nickel in the basket and, with the cunning of a carnival trickster, pulled out a fistful of quarters. After church, like a big-hearted benefactor, he bought five-cent ice cream cones or penny candy for us all.

We'd walk home after morning service for an early Sunday dinner that was cooked and waiting on the stove. We hurried back for a three o'clock afternoon music service, and then BTU (Baptist Training Unit) started at six o'clock. If there was a funeral, the Sunday marathon could go on until nine at night. Daddy had rules (never fully explained) about what we could or could not do on Sundays: we couldn't iron clothes; could only listen to church music on the radio; and we couldn't go to the movies. When the weather permitted and there was no three o'clock musical service at the church, we walked to Union Station and watched people board the trains, dressed in their travel finery. The added attraction for me was the block-long sculpture fountain across Market Street from the train station. Water sprayed from the mouths of fish, some of which were held by anatomically complete bronze nudes.

Daddy was a busy man who assigned little importance to connecting the correct names of his children to the appropriate child, especially the girls. We scurried around the church on Sundays trying to avoid him, but sometimes he would catch a glimpse of one of us and give us some task to do. We were accustomed to his rapid, rhythmic roll call: "Vern-Beverly-Jean-Tootie-Vivian!" We always stood frozen, waiting for his amused exasperation at his futile attempts. Then he would beckon with one sharp flick of his closed fingers and say with a chuckle, "Come here, girl." It was an infrequent opportunity to openly laugh at and with Daddy.

As in many other households, we always had boarders, more commonly called "roomers." My mother's "business box" was a gray, galvanized metal box with a broken locking mechanism that housed all our family bills, receipts, contracts, and other important documents. I inherited this, and over the years I would occasionally pull the business box from the back shelf of my closet and notice something new among the rent and mortgage receipts, W-2 forms, and pay stubs that went back to when my parents were first married. One surprising find were my father's 1952 report cards from music classes at the St. Louis Music and Arts College. In 1952 my father had eight children and three jobs. Amazingly, he was also attending music fundamentals, piano, and voice classes at night.

Among the tightly packed, faded envelopes and creased papers was a little blue book with carbon copies of rent receipts from 1952 through 1954. My grandmother rented out a room in our basement for five dollars a week, and a front room on the second floor for seven dollars. All the yellowed receipts were in my grandmother's name, but written in my mother's handwriting. Another of Mama's responsibilities was apparently to act as rent collector for her mother-in-law.

The second-floor renter was Mr. Aaron Powell; he was a slightly built and neatly dressed man who wore a tan felt fedora. He sat outside on the front steps on warm evenings talking to Mama through the open window in our front room. He would smoke one last cigarette before retiring to his nonsmoking room across the hall from my grandmother's bedroom and kitchen.

The basement rental receipts were made out to three women during that time frame: Ester Phillips, Ruthie Booker, and Augusta Logan. These roomers may have been domestic workers who had come up from the South and "lived on the place" where they worked. They had every other weekend off and rented the front basement room so as to have a bed for sleeping and a place to store their meager possessions. Some of the dates were different weeks in the same month, so it's likely the room was shared by the women on alternating weekends.

If there were a place to keep out the wind and the rain, apparently my grandmother would rent it out. One such renter in need of shelter was a gentle, sweet soul we children called Miss Lit'l Bit.

The coal shed was a wooden and tar paper structure off the alley in our backyard with a partitioned front section where we stored tools, wheelbarrows, and old trunks. The rear part was where coal, used to fuel our stoves, was shoveled from a flatbed truck through a chute in the alley. I don't know where Miss Lit'l Bit lived before Mama noticed her leaving the shed early one morning. And I never questioned how she lived inside the dark shed without water or electricity. At first, Mama ignored Lit'l Bit's comings and goings through the alley gate. Then one day she had my brothers move the things stored in the half room to a place under Grandmama's back steps and covered them with a heavy, oil-stained canvas tarp.

Miss Lit'l Bit was a tiny dark-skinned woman with short pomaded hair brushed back to lay close to her scalp. She was quiet, deferential, and kept to herself most of the time—except early on Saturday evenings when she drank. On those evenings, Lit'l Bit's eyes narrowed and her closed lips stretched wide into an impish smile as she danced in the backyard. Her knees bobbed, and her head followed her shoulders as she swayed from side to side. Sometimes she waved her arms in unaware grace, like a ragged princess prancing in her loose-fitting cotton dress to the music she alone heard. Mama watched from the kitchen window as we giggled and joined in, imitating Lit'l Bit's teetering movements. The weekend displays that Mama may have seen as sad but harmless placed Lit'l Bit at the top of my grandmother's list of despised people. The quiet merriment never lasted long before Bit, as Mama called her, retreated into the shed.

I don't know where she went when she walked down the alley early in the morning. But months after her presence was first known, then accepted, things started looking up for her. Per the rent receipts, for most of 1954 a woman named Ester Phillips rented a room in our basement. I think Ester and Miss Lit'l Bit were one and the same. When I started kindergarten, Mama worked as a temporary part-time bookkeeper during the busy season at the toy factory a few blocks up the alley from our house, and she allowed Miss Lit'l Bit to watch Ferman until our older siblings got home from school.

Even though the door to her basement room was under a makeshift plywood cover on the front of our house, Miss Lit'l Bit continued to enter and leave our yard through the back gate off the alley.

"You still here?" It was the question directed at the darker-than-the-rest face nodding toward a bowl of cornflakes and chewing slowly. Mama was making one of her periodic surprise morning inspections just to make sure everyone was doing what they were supposed to do before school. March looked up with his eyes, barely rotating his head, and said, "Yes, ma'am."

Two evenings earlier, after football practice, Mama had noticed March seated in the same position, hunched over a bowl of pinto beans, ham hocks, and cornbread. Randle asked if his friend March could spend the night. "If it's alright with his mother," Mama said casually.

"She don't care," March responded.

After March spent a few more mornings and evenings at our house, Mama went over to Washington Technical High School to inquire about this boy who had been sleeping in our basement. She learned that his full name was Norman March. The school counselor called his foster mother and put my mother on the phone. It turned out March had left the foster home months earlier with an older brother who had aged out of the system. He was eating and sleeping wherever he could, but was still attending school. March became the ninth child in our family for the next three years.

He joined the ranks of teenage boys on Bernard Street who went to school, played football in the fall, and roamed the neighborhood doing who-knows-what on weekends. March talked low and slow to mask his stutter. He had a toothless half-smile mostly reserved for Mama and was skilled at staying out of Daddy's sight. For a while, I'm not sure if Daddy even knew that he lived with us. He helped clean the church after school and on Saturday afternoons with us: sweeping, mopping, emptying trash, dusting the pews and the chairs in the pulpit. But when our whole family filed out for church on Sunday mornings, March stayed in the basement. Sometimes he went to see his mother, who still lived in the house from which the state had removed him and his siblings years before. He was always back in time to eat dinner when we returned home from church.

March worked weekends and summers stocking shelves and delivering groceries at a store on Leland Avenue in University City. Like Daddy, he left early for work and came home in the evenings. He bought his school clothes and sometimes brought home Hostess cupcakes for everybody. On Saturdays, when he got paid, Ferman and I waited for him on the curb in front of our house for our payday treat: MoonPies that March hid behind his back before presenting them to us with his shy smile. His next stop was Mama, to whom he dutifully handed a modest portion of his pay.

Norman March slipped into our family and became another older brother and Randle's best friend. On high school graduation day, Mama watched March walk across the stage and receive his diploma in a suit he had bought for himself. Randle wasn't there; he had gotten suspended from school for fighting and had joined the Marines. When March couldn't find a job in the printing trade that he had learned in school, he decided to follow Randle into the military. But not before, at Beverly's encouragement, he backed Daddy's one-and-only-ever car out of the driveway and crashed it into a tree. Daddy displayed remarkable restraint when he told March, "Son, it's time for you to leave."

March joined the Air Force that summer and disappeared from our family life as slyly as he had entered it. At first, Mama got a few letters and a picture of him looking handsome in his uniform, then nothing—he was gone.

Years later, Mama was sitting and crocheting on the large front porch at our new house on Oakley Place. A familiar sight, she skillfully pulled the white cotton thread from a spool with one hand and wound it around her index finger for tension. With her other hand, she hooked, looped, and knotted the thread with a crochet needle, creating intricate lace doilies that cascaded and heaped into her lap. As she worked, a car pulled up in front and a tall man with his head slightly lowered walked up the steps and said, cautiously, "Hi, Mama."

She looked up. "M-a-r-c-h, boy," she said with a happy lilt. "Where have you been?"

March sat on the wide concrete steps at her feet and began to answer Mama's question.

"I was in the military for six years, and I should have stayed there. It was the first time I had more food than I could eat, a bed of my own, and a job that I was good at. I had money to drink and gamble with." Chuckling, he said, "And on the first and fifteenth of the month I got paid again. Mama, the worst decision I ever made was to get out of the military and come back to St. Louis. I couldn't find a decent job, and the drinking and gambling almost put me right back on the streets."

He cleared his throat and lowered his eyes to the familiar dance of her tapered fingers before continuing. "A friend and I robbed a barbecue joint in East St. Louis and we got caught. I spent sixteen months in jail." He straightened his back slightly, as if relieved he had said what he came to say. Their eyes met as they talked about other things: where he lived, how good he looked, did he have children? He smiled that half-smile as he assured, "I got a job delivering packages now, and I hear they're hiring at the packing house in East St. Louis." Awkwardly he added, "I ran into Beverly a few weeks ago, and the first thing she said was, 'You ought to go see Mama.' So here I am. I'm sorry it took me so long."

I saw March periodically throughout the years. He kept in contact with Beverly and for a while he was the UPS delivery guy in the office where I worked.

Many years later, when he was in his late seventies, I contacted March to read him the story I had written about him; he provided details about his life before and after he lived with us. I asked what he remembered most about the time he spent with our family. In a warm, low voice that still sounded familiar after decades, he said, "I remember that Mama was so pretty, and I was so grateful that she took me in."

THREE

The punishment for continuing to talk at nap time after Miss Arnold had reminded you to be quiet was to sit on the floor in the chair-opening beneath her large wooden desk. That's where I was on June 6, 1955, when Jean and Tootie came to my first-grade classroom at Lincoln Elementary School and whispered something to our teacher. They removed the chair that blocked the opening, leaned down, and reached in unison to pull me out and up. Before I could ask how they knew I needed rescuing from my wooden cell, they said in unison, "Daddy's in the hospital."

They tugged me along the shellacked brown cork floors, down the long, wide corridor of classrooms, and through the tall double doors that opened onto Eugenia Street. The street looked different when just three little girls walked in front of the school and along the dark-green painted iron fence. The schoolyard looked bigger too, with no children playing in it. They pulled my arms in front of me as I trotted to keep up with their long strides.

"What happened to Daddy?" I asked.

Jean shot back her answer without breaking her stride: "He got hit by a truck."

At that moment I became aware that we were standing on a street corner while my sisters' heads pivoted from side to side, looking for cars and trucks before we stepped into the street.

We walked a block in silence and turned the corner at Jefferson Avenue where we saw Miss Cora standing in the doorway of the Barcelona Tavern, as Mama had told Jean she would be. Miss Cora, who was also Tootie's godmother, opened her arms and gently pressed our faces together and against her body. She ushered us through the intersection with her arms stretched wide, a crossing guard in a pink waitress uniform complete with little white apron. Safely on the west side of Jefferson, she instructed us to change out of our school clothes and stay in the house until our mother got home.

We were used to Mama being there when we came home from school. It was mid-afternoon, but the house was dark, and the familiar background sound of Mama's soap operas was missing. Vern arrived next, then Beverly with Ferman in tow; Honey soon followed, and finally Randle. There was none of the usual chatter. We still had little information, and since we didn't know what to think, we didn't talk.

A standing rule in our house was that if Mama was not home when we got in from school, somebody had better start cooking. So Vern went to the kitchen. Guided by the stout butcher-wrapped package sitting front and center in the refrigerator, she made her version of one of our favorite meals: beans and franks. The "franks" portions of the meal could be wieners, canned Vienna sausages, even Spam. But on a good day, the franks were big fat Polish sausages. Vern was a good cook, and she had a knack for seasoning ordinary foods to make them special. She stretched the two long links and three large cans of Campbell's Pork and Beans into a hearty meal for eight hungry kids. She sliced the smoked sausages into quarter-size medallions and browned them in a large skillet with chopped onions. To the flavorless beige beans she added catsup for color, red pepper for zip, and enough cane syrup to make us forget we were eating canned beans. A few slices of Wonder Bread and a glass of red Kool-Aid made it a special school-night treat. She set aside a portion for Daddy, then we filled assorted plates and bowls and fanned out to our eating spots: the back steps, the side of a bottom bunk bed, or leaning against the kitchen sink. Ferman and I sat in the limited space at our small kitchen table.

It was dark outside when Mama finally got home to tell us that Daddy had been hit by a truck while repairing the streetcar tracks on South Broadway. The driver kept going as Daddy lay in the street with a crushed left leg and his right ear nearly torn off. The ambulance first took him to the emergency room at City Hospital No. 1 on Lafayette Street, where they set his leg in a cast, sutured his ear, and stabilized his neck with sandbags. He was later transferred to People's Hospital on Locust Street, which was a segregated hospital for colored people, not far from our house.

A few days later a bus driver who had witnessed the accident reported the license number of the truck. It was owned and driven by a fifty-six-year-old pretzel vendor who wore thick glasses. He was arrested and identified as the man who had hit another pedestrian six months earlier.

Daddy was in the hospital for three months while his severely damaged leg and ear healed. The sandbags protecting his neck were replaced with a padded white neck brace. On Sundays after church, we walked over Jefferson, past Market Street a few blocks to Locust, then down to Twenty-Third Street. Mama went into the hospital, and shortly after, Daddy would appear at the second-floor window. We waved, jumped up and down, and yelled, "Hi Daddy!" for a few minutes, then turned and walked back home. Mama would follow later with Daddy's dirty laundry and a small bag of goodies that he accumulated over each week while he was in the hospital. Opening Daddy's stash was like Christmas. There were boxes of tissues, small bars of soap, small tubes of toothpaste, and little bottles of body lotion. Sometimes there were peppermint or black licorice candies that people had brought him, but my favorite were the tiny individual packs of sugar.

Sometimes Mama would dole out the envelopes of sugar like prizes for us to sprinkle over our oatmeal, corn flakes, or buttered toast. Occasionally, when no one was around, I pilfered the packages and let the crystals flow from the torn openings into little mounds on my outstretched tongue, closing my eyes as the sweetness melted in my mouth. One night, feeling confident that my thievery went unnoticed, I sneaked a handful of the treasures under my bedcovers and, in the dark, quietly filled my mouth with sugar. Hours later my gurgling, cramping stomach was relieved in an eruption of oozing warmth inside my pajama bottoms. I slipped out of my soiled pajamas, pushed them aside, and climbed the ladder at the end of our bed to snuggle beside Tootie in the top bunk. As she reached behind to pull me closer to her in the narrow bed, her hand landed on my sticky, stinky, bare bottom. She paused momentarily, withdrew her hand to her nose, and realized in her sleepiness what had happened. At the end of a long, piercing "EEEEEEE," she screamed, "MAMAAAA!"

The next time we visited Daddy, he yelled from the second-floor window that there would be no more sugar packets for me.

Daddy's job was "a good job for a colored man." We knew this because he told us so often. His job took him far beyond the cultural boundaries of Mill Creek. He went to work early to "drink coffee and shoot the breeze with the white fellas at work." We hardly ever saw these almost mythical white fellas. They were shadowy figures behind the wheel of a pickup truck that sometimes dropped Daddy off with big bushel baskets of sweet potatoes, corn, tomatoes, or squash that they grew on farms in St. Charles or some other faraway county we had never heard of. Other times the truck would pause at the corner of our street just long enough for Daddy to jump out and pull from it burlap sacks that were too heavy to carry on his regular streetcar ride home. The sacks were sagging with skinned rabbits and possums, and deer meat from weekend hunting trips. The other men never got out of the truck, so I didn't really know what a white fella looked like.

Daddy's job was steady work with overtime pay in the winter when it snowed, and he worked from 4:00 a.m. to 6:00 p.m. clearing snow and salting streets. He got two weeks vacation that he took just before Christmas so he could work as a seasonal worker sorting and bagging mail at the main post office during the holiday rush. And there were health and disability benefits that paid for his time off after the accident.

After thirteen months of hospitalization and recuperation, Daddy returned to work with a pronounced limp, a mangled ear, and the promise of an even "better job" as one of the first black truck drivers for the St. Louis Public Service Company. He and Mama had spent an evening sitting on the side of their bed, using the hard-sided suitcase as a writing surface, and completing documents required for him to return to work. The next day he took Ferman and me on a streetcar ride to the Public Service Offices on Park Avenue. After turning in his paperwork, we walked a few blocks to the truck garage on Thirty-Ninth Street, behind the Pevely Milk plant on Grand Avenue near Chouteau.

The garage had doors that were bigger than our house and trucks with tires that were taller than my brother and me. Men in bib overalls and oil-stained coveralls greeted Daddy with slapping handshakes and pats on his back. While Ferman stared slack-jawed at the big red trucks, I searched the faces of the men, wondering if these were "the white fellas" that Daddy talked about—because they didn't look *white* to me.

When the greetings slowed, my father palmed my and my brother's heads with his fingers spread wide apart, rotating Ferman's butter-colored face away from the trucks that he had not taken his eyes off of since we entered the garage. "These are my two youngest," Daddy said by way of introduction. The men looked down at us, there was a long pause, then a man with a red face that looked bumpy and itchy said, "Damn, Ross, you must have a beautiful wife." Then they all looked around at each other and laughed loudly. Daddy laughed too, but not as loud or as long as the white fellas at work. I didn't know what was so funny about what the red-faced-white-fella said, but I agreed with him: Daddy did have a beautiful wife.

The next week Daddy started his new job driving one of those big red trucks, and Ferman couldn't have been happier than when Daddy would swing by when his route brought him close to home, and let us climb up into the cab, sit on his lap, and grab the steering wheel.

We ran up and down the sidewalk for the rest of the afternoon with outstretched arms, gyrating our pretend steering wheel and growling the sound of a revving motor.

Daddy had never owned a car but was now driving a one-and-a half-ton truck, hauling trash from St. Louis Public Service Company facilities around the city. His new job took him away from the dangerous work of cleaning and repairing streetcar tracks in the center lanes of the busiest streets in the city. It was not only a better paying job, but it gave him the relative freedom to veer a few blocks from his designated route at will.

The Wonder Bread Thrift Store that sold day-old bread was near his truck route. He used to get off the bus on his way home on Wednesdays to buy ten loaves of bread. In his new job, he'd leave his big red truck idling in front of the store while he ran inside for our weekly supply.

There were other significant perks to Daddy's new job. Trash dumpsters in municipal transportation offices, garages, and construction sites were treasure troves for a resourceful man like my father. Partially used notepads, logoed three-ring binders, sheets of carbon paper, and pencils with erasers were welcome additions to our school supplies. Generous lengths of scrap-lumber were stored in the cab of his truck; nails and screws that had littered the workshop floors were swept up and tossed into a waiting coffee can behind his driver's seat.

Oil filters removed from city buses were the ideal size to fit into the belly of our wood-burning stove. The smell of burning engine oil permeated our house. The filters burned so hotly that the heat buckled and eventually burned through the metal flue pipe leading to the chimney.

People discarded all kinds of things to which Daddy gave new life and purpose: an incomplete and tattered set of *Childcraft* encyclopedias, a box of records that included a three-album set of Tennessee Ernie Ford music in its original reinforced cardboard case. I listened to and sang along loudly—"Sixteen tons and what do you get? Another day older and deeper in debt!"—for months after Daddy eventually brought home a used portable record player for us to play our newly acquired music collection. Mama's favorite was "You'll Never Walk Alone," sung by Roy Hamilton, the only black singer among the gently used records. He had an elegant tenor voice, and it didn't hurt that his last name was the same as her maiden name.

One day Daddy swung by home on his lunch hour and dropped off two half-empty five-gallon cans of yellow paint typically used to paint traffic lanes down the middle of streets or to designate no-parking zones on curbs

I don't know what Daddy's intentions were for the paint, except for the usual rationale that "it was too good to throw away." But at some point, it was decided that our kitchen would benefit from a little brightening up. When we asked, "Can we?" Mama's reliable response was, as always, "Sure."

The dried skin halfway down each bucket was peeled away to reveal thick, smooth, sunflower yellow paint. Randle was in charge. He and Honey dragged in the ladder from the shed, covered the cabinets, stove, and sink with newspaper, and painted the ceiling and upper sections of the walls. I took turns with Jean and Tootie, sharing a single brush to splatter, spread, and smear paint over every dingy inch of the lower walls. When the kitchen was transformed by the garish shock of color, and there was still paint left to spread, we looked around for something else to brighten.

We pulled our clunky wooden bunk beds to the middle of the floor, rolled and removed the thin mattresses, and covered the drab and dinged bed frames in the vibrant hue that Mama laughingly dubbed "Middle of the Road Yellow."

Mama's name for the paint we'd spread far and wide, like many of her casual utterances, soon reflected her keener insight. At night, when the lights were off, the window shades were raised high, and the moon was full, our beds glowed in the dark.

FOUR

Honey was only nine or ten when he figured out how to contribute to the household coffers. Daddy would often exclaim in the midst of his big baritone laugh, "That boy sho' know how to make money." Running errands for our neighbor, Mrs. Thigpen, doing chores for Grandmama, and collecting empty soda bottles for the penny refunds was good enough to buy candy and Archie comic books, but Honey had more ambitious plans in mind.

He saw Randle's friend James Price pulling a wooden wagon filled with copies of the evening *St. Louis Post-Dispatch* every day after school. James lived on the east side of Jefferson where it intersected with Bernard Street. Crossing Jefferson Avenue to get to James's house placed Honey outside of his nine-year-old perimeter. Besides, James was in eighth grade. But Honey watched him race past all the other kids at a full sprint every afternoon when school was out. By the time other neighborhood kids meandered across the Jefferson Bridge, Roosevelt Ferguson peeled off at Scott Street, the Lattimores at Randolph, and the Ross kids turned the corner at Bernard— their minds on shooting marbles and jumping double-dutch after school—James had already begun his lucrative paper route.

He parked his weathered wagon at the curb while he ran in and out of small businesses and the houses of regular subscribers along Washington Avenue and Pine and Market Streets. He knocked on the doors of customers in century-old two-family brick houses on Spruce, Walnut, and Clark, leaving a neatly folded paper just inside their screen doors. He was in perpetual motion while dropping nickels and dimes in his sagging pockets from random customers at bus stops, restaurants, and barber shops. James's self-confidence and sense of purpose were apparent, and Honey wanted to emulate him.

Honey knew how to be around older boys: walk behind them, don't talk, and run when they say run. Honey admired Randle, with whom he shared the top bunk bed every night. He willingly accepted routine glancing slaps on the back of the head for the privilege of tagging along when Randle barked from a few steps ahead, "C'mon boy." But James Price was a little different from the other thirteen-year-olds boys, so Honey took a chance and asked him if he could help deliver papers after school. To his delight and surprise, James said yes.

The next day after school, Honey sprinted in the wake of air behind James to a dimly lit warehouse just west of Jefferson on Washington. There, an unsmiling white-haired man sat smoking a cigar behind a beat-up wooden desk with a clipboard in front of him and surrounded by stacks of newspapers. Along the wall, a row of high-sided oak wagons with a sheen of dark patina, big iron wheels, and long curved metal handles leaned one against another, like big brown dominoes stopped in mid-fall. Just before leaving the bright sunlight for the dark, cool warehouse, James had looked back at Honey and said, "Don't. Say. Nothing." Honey had not even asked how much James would pay him. His goal was to have one of those three-foot-long, metal-trimmed wooden wagons of his own. It didn't take long. James was a thorough trainer who patiently demonstrated how to configure the papers for easy retrieval. He even taught Honey how to handle the occasional robber: "Split your money up in all your pockets. When they come up to you, don't say nothing, just give them the money from your front right pocket." Our brother Randle could have given Honey that same advice because paperboys in other neighborhoods were often Randle's victims.

James soon gave Honey the residential portion of his paper route. That way James could spend more time delivering to commercial businesses along Market Street and professional offices in the People's Finance Building, where he could sell more papers in fewer locations.

Honey left papers at homes where most customers worked during the week, so he had to return on Saturdays to collect his money. That gave his customers an opportunity to meet, chat with, and serve cold water and lemonade to "that polite Ross boy" who delivered their papers. Though his given name was Shepperd, after our pastor, his golden-brown complexion and sweet disposition left no doubt about the genesis of this nickname. Honey was that kid the teachers favored, old ladies smiled at, and to whom old men told jokes.

Every Saturday afternoon before Christmas, Honey's empty paper wagon would be filled with boxes of homemade cookies, cakes, and candy. And best of all, his pockets were filled with enough silver dollars to rival Daddy's weekly paycheck. And just like Daddy did every Friday evening, Honey proudly dropped his remunerations into Mama's ample lap.

———

My parents never had adult friends or neighbors inside our house: there was no place for anyone to sit, and very little standing room. Our furnishings consisted of beds, chests of drawers, chifforobes, an upright piano, and the two used televisions that had to be turned on at the same time to get both picture and sound. But that didn't mean they lacked for friends. Their primary relationships outside the family were at their separate churches—Mama's more subdued Christian Methodist Episcopal and Daddy's spirited Baptist. Over time, Mama was church secretary, board trustee, vacation Bible school teacher, and belonged to multiple clubs and committees at her church. She volunteered at our schools, the NAACP membership drives, and Red Cross blood drives. She looked so professional when she wore the blue cotton twill uniform when she was paid to work at blood drives twice a month.

Her array of women friends were barmaids, domestics, teachers, entrepreneurs, and housewives. What many of them had in common was that they were all childless and many became our godmothers: Aunt Daisy, Miss Savannah, Miss Cora, and Uncle Bennie's second wife, Wildry. Wildry would half-jokingly say, "Frances, you ought to give me Tootie, she looks just like me." Mama's deadpan reply: "I'll happily lend you Tootie for the afternoon, even a weekend, but she'd need to be back home by Sunday after church."

These loving ladies bought us gifts. We spent the night at their homes—which were so much nicer than ours—and they endured our holiday programs at school and church. These were the same women who adorned their houses with the doilies, tablecloths, bedspreads, and curtains that were produced by the perpetual motion of my mother's hands.

Aunt Mary and Uncle Clarence, my godparents, had moved out of Mill Creek years before. Aunt Mary worked as a domestic five days a week and only came home on weekends to cook, clean, do laundry, and go to church. One of my older siblings would put me on the Vandeventer bus to ride north across town every other Saturday to spend the day with Aunt Mary. Uncle Clarence would be standing on the corner of Vandeventer and St. Louis Avenue dressed in a suit with a starched white shirt that Aunt Mary had freshly ironed for him that morning. I don't know why, but in his fedora hat that matched his suit, he was a fixture on that corner, like Perlmutter's Department Store, Kirkland's Dry Cleaners, and Stone's Drug Store. He was there every day, telling stories about going to the Kentucky Derby to people who stopped to chat. He chuckled low and slow at his own jokes without showing his teeth. When I jumped off the bus, he'd greet me with, "Hey little rascal," and walk with me down St. Louis Avenue to the middle of the block, unlock their front door to let me in, then return to the corner.

Aunt Mary and Uncle Clarence had no children. She and Mama were friends from church, but they could not be more different. Mama could be relaxed and friendly while Aunt Mary was serious and regimented. Everything in Aunt Mary's home was neat, clean, starched, and polished. Most all of her furnishings were given to her by her longtime employer after they redecorated. The softly rounded edges of her bed were like clouds covered in a white chenille bedspread. The fringe along the bottom of the bedspread hovered above the cleanest linoleum floor I'd ever seen. And there was nothing under the bed, except Uncle Clarence's tan leather slippers. A solitary light-blue lamp sat on each night table beside the bed, framed by lace-curtained windows. The dark wood dresser had carved edges and legs and a mirror that tilted slightly forward, reflecting an image of pretty bottles and a glass cellar filled with fragrant dusting power. In the living room, on each end of the sofa, were polished tables with milky white porcelain lamps on brass pedestals that sat on starched doilies my mother had crocheted. There were glass figurines and ashtrays, and candy dishes with crunchy, white sugar ovals filled with a black-licorice-flavored jelly.

Aunt Mary and I spent most of our time together in her bright kitchen. I'd wash my hands in the small bathroom that had a slanted ceiling to accommodate the stairs that led to the landlady's apartment on the second floor. There were embroidered hand towels hanging on a rack near the sink like the ones my mother stitched by the dozens to sell just before Christmas. I knew they were for show, so I'd use the towel hanging on the back of the door to dry my hands.

As usual, I carefully set the kitchen table for lunch the way Aunt Mary had taught me, using her matching dishes and flatware. Her instructions would end with, "Remember the glass sits just above the knife." We ate sandwiches that she'd cut in half, potato salad, corn on the cob, or my favorite, deviled eggs. And we drank lemonade or iced tea with a slice of lemon floating on top.

When lunch was over, she'd let me scoop and measure the Swans Down cake flour and sugar for pound cakes. After blending the flour and sugar with the butter and eggs, she'd cradle the large mixing bowl in the crook of one arm and aerate the batter with rapid strokes of the wooden spoon until it peaked like thick meringue. When the cake pan was filled, I'd lick the fluffy golden sweetness from the spoon and mixing bowl.

In the summer we'd sit on the back porch and snap string beans, or shell pecans for pies. Even her backyard was pretty, with grass on both sides of a paved walkway that stretched all the way to the alley, and rose bushes that were carefully spaced to hide the simple wire fence.

Sometimes Uncle Clarence would come in when it was about time for me to get back on the bus and go home. He'd heavily pat the top of my head and say, "Hey, little rascal, wha'cha up to?" Then he'd disappear into the small half-room off the kitchen that had a twin bed, a straight-back wooden chair, and an old floor-model radio where he'd listen to horse races and baseball games.

I wanted to spend the night, sleep in that cozy half-room, and listen to the radio all by myself. But neither Mama nor I trusted my "small bladder" to hold through the night.

So at Mama's prompting, whenever Aunt Mary invited me to sleep over on Saturday night and go to church with her on Sunday morning, I smiled timidly and said, "No, thank you." I could see the disappointment on her face when she said, "Maybe next time."

In June of 1955, I completed my first year of school at Lincoln Elementary. One month earlier, the bond issue put forth by Mayor Raymond R. Tucker passed and set in motion plans to demolish our neighborhood. But it would be another three years before any significant change would register on my consciousness. In 1955 I remained blissfully unaware of the wider world.

I routinely skipped past the stately brick wall that enclosed the Trotters's small front yard, and Mrs. Thigpin's (we called her Miss Stickpin) washed stone steps that we were not allowed to sit on. I could always hear the television through the screen door at Jerry Rigney's house. His house was next to the field of sunflowers where preteen boys cut the long spiny stalks and played swashbuckling pirates for hours on end. I had walked the one long block east from our house on Bernard to Jefferson Avenue many times, but was not allowed to go any farther without supervision. So the walk to school each morning and back home each afternoon was a daily adventure for me.

Back in September, my sister Tootie, who was starting third grade, had led the way as my next-door neighbor Clem Trotter and I got to turn the corner at Jefferson Avenue. We walked toward Spruce, passed Bath House No. 5, which my grandmother called "the colored bathhouse" and where everybody except me had learned to swim. We crossed Clark toward Cou'in Brownie's house, where my sisters and I got our hair straightened, then curled. I'd walked as far as Market Street with my mother before to shop at the dense knot of small fruit markets, shoe and clothing stores, and used furniture stores. But to get to my school each day, we had to go across Jefferson Avenue. I relished the independence of peeling off from my older sisters and brothers, who attended a different school, and going in the opposite direction at Jefferson with Tootie and Clem. We walked to the corner of Eugenia Street where Miss Cora was starting her shift at the Barcelona Tavern. She would stand in the doorway of the tavern and wave as we passed and proceeded another short block to Walnut Street. There, the sixth-grade crossing guard waved us across to the east side of Jefferson, where the three-story brick school building loomed large to my eager eyes.

The three middle Ross children turned south at Jefferson and meandered in small groups of friends across the Jefferson Bridge. The sand and rock concrete sidewalk and shoulder-high walls of the bridge stretched a quarter-mile across the Mill Creek Valley train yard and ended at Chouteau Avenue. In single file, the school children would double back beneath the bridge at Chouteau for another short block to reach Attucks Elementary School on Papin Street.

The two oldest Ross kids took different paths to school. LaVern went west, to Vashon High, where she was an "A" student, and Randle to Washington Technical High School on Nineteenth and Franklin, where he learned offset printing and perfected his tough-guy image. Ferman, the youngest, was three and a half and now had Mama all to himself.

I loved going to school— I had my very own little wooden chair and three new friends who shared the sturdy oak table that was just the right size for our five-year-old bodies. I adored crayons and pencils and colored paper, standing in lines, raising my hand, and the afternoon snack of graham crackers and milk. Most of all, I loved playing tag in the huge schoolyard with more friends than I had ever had. My favorite new friend was Janice Compton. I think she liked school even more than me. Janice smiled all the time; her cocoa-colored eyes lit up with the slightest eye contact, and she could not keep still. She came to school in her dirty "play" clothes. Some days she didn't even wear socks. Best of all, she didn't have to get her hair combed every morning either.

Janice didn't cross Jefferson Avenue like Clem and me to get to school. One day we stood on the bottom crossbar of the iron fence in the back of the school playground and pointed to where she lived. We couldn't see her house, but she said, "I walk through that vacant lot with the tall weeds and then down the hill to the railroad tracks to get home."

I told my mother about Janice, and that she could see the trains go by from her house. Mama calmly reminded me, "Those train tracks are dangerous, and I don't want you to *ever* leave the schoolyard with Janice to go see where she lives." When I told my sister Beverly about Janice, she said, "Janice is poor, and the people who live down that hill live in shacks, and their toilets are outside." Some kids were mean and wouldn't play with her. But I liked Janice, and she liked me. I wanted to wear my dirty "play" clothes to school just like her.

Janice was always happy to talk about anything, and filled every pause in the conversation with a story, a suggestion of a game to play, or notes on whatever random thing was going on in her life. One day she interrupted a lull by telling us that she and her brother slept in the same bed with her mother and father. We laughed when Janice bounced up and down while rotating her midsection to show us how their bed shook at night. She said her parents made funny noises and would be out of breath like they were running in a race. I laughed when I relayed Janice's story to my mother after school. Mama didn't laugh; she just cleared her throat and nodded her head.

It wasn't unusual for Janice to miss a day at school. But after a while, when she didn't come for a few days, Clem Trotter sat in her chair at our table. When she came back to school, she was in a different class and played at recess in a different part of the schoolyard. Sometimes we waved at each other when we were standing in line to go to our separate classrooms. She got excited and smiled when she saw me and waved her skinny arms wildly so that I couldn't miss seeing her.

————————

Saturday mornings started a little later than school days, but not by much. Grandmama and Daddy were still the first to rise, and their early stirs were familiar. From my bunk bed, I could hear the smooth bottoms of Grandmama's house shoes slide just before the shift of her weight made the floorboards creak beneath the thin layer of linoleum. Then came the smell of coffee. Next, I could hear Daddy climb the steps that started just outside the front room where he and Mama slept. He visited his mother every Saturday morning. Daddy was her only child, and their bond was close and comfortable as they shared breakfast once a week in her small kitchen. She sipped strong coffee, and he drank a large glass of buttermilk. She piled his plate with hot biscuits, sweet apple or peach preserves, and thick slices of smoked ham fried until crusty brown, then simmered in coffee to make red-eye gravy. There was little urgency in their weekly visits, and the muffled sound of Daddy's baritone voice as he laughed intermittently reminded me it was Saturday.

After their short ritual, the morning atmosphere changed when Daddy descended the stairs with an armful of clean laundry his mother had washed and folded for him. He opened the door leading to the basement and hollered down to where my brothers slept: "Honey, get up and get ready to go to Soulard with your grandmama!" Shortly after, Honey rounded the corner from the basement stairwell, then took two steps at a time to Grandmama's rooms on the second floor. He knew leftover biscuits, cooked fruit, and ham were waiting for him too.

Grandmama had designated and predictable apparel for the days of her life. On workdays she donned a modest brown felt hat with a rolled brim. Her Sunday hat was black velvet with a rhinestone brooch and a curved feather. There were house dresses and gardening dresses that were worn for years at a higher status. But on Saturdays, when she took two streetcars to Soulard Farmers Market, she wanted to be respectable yet practical. Her hair was covered in a floral print cotton scarf gathered snugly to the front and rolled like a fat cigar just above her forehead. Her cotton print shirtwaist dress had large pockets for her coin purse, a handkerchief, two peppermint candies, and a pocketknife. Comfortable black oxfords were paired with opaque brown cotton stockings rolled and knotted just below her knees.

All of her grandchildren took turns accompanying her to Soulard Market, but Honey was her most willing helper. The centuries-old location that stretched from Seventh Street to Ninth Street had a grand Italian Renaissance-style front entrance on Lafayette Street, flanked by two elegant green spaces on both sides of a long walkway. A phalanx of Saturday shoppers converged and paraded through the arched arcade of stalls piled high with fresh produce, smoked meats, fragrant ground spices, and poultry. But Grandmama and Honey, or whichever assistant was trailing behind her that day, veered from the crowded path to the open space in the rear of the market along Carrol Street. There, a row of trucks loaded with farmers' weekly harvests filled spaces at daybreak. Grandmama and Honey joined a small group of other foragers who arrived early before the heat and flies.

When the farmers stacked pyramiding displays of fruits and vegetables for their meandering customers, they threw bruised and imperfect produce into large wooden bins behind their stalls. Without a word between them, Honey unfurled four homemade flour-sack bags he carried under his arm. He slid three of the empty bags over his wrist and with the skill of a well-practiced catcher, he held an open sack to the side of Grandmama's flexing elbow as she surveyed the bins, retrieved her pocketknife, and proceeded to carve away bruises, wilt, or rot. Then she gingerly placed her choices into Honey's well-positioned receptacles.

When all four bags were filled, they exited the rear of the market with bags full of purposely pared fruits and vegetables. In her neat head scarf, practical dress, and sensible shoes, she looked just like all the other shoppers. While waiting at the curb for the next streetcar, Grandmama would reach into her pocket and share her peppermint candy.

Most of the people in Mill Creek were black except for the owners of the corner grocery stores, the shops on Market Street, and the few Chinese people we only saw inside their restaurants, like the one whose plate glass window read "King Hong Cafe." The stylized red pagoda above the lettering could easily have been mistaken for a crown. But no one called Mr. Hong's, or any other of the half-dozen Chinese takeout restaurants in Mill Creek, by the names painted on the windows. They were all off-handedly, and without ill-intent, called "the Chinaman's," a term commonly used to identify people of Chinese descent from the time they arrived in America to work on the transcontinental railroad. "Chinaman's" was also a catch-all label for the businesses they operated. The Chinatown district between Seventh and Tenth streets and Chestnut and Walnut, called Hop Alley, had been there since the 1860s. The rundown buildings on either side of the alley were homes and businesses owned by Chinese immigrants who operated hand laundries, tea shops, spice shops, and restaurants. There were often stories in the *St. Louis Post-Dispatch* that warned of violent crimes and opium dens within the insular enclave.

By the 1930s, younger generations slowly migrated to adjacent poor and black communities to open small restaurants. There, they sold inexpensive meals in white cardboard boxes that passed through small openings in walls haphazardly erected to divide bustling, steamy, and fragrant kitchens from waiting customers. A number scribbled on a small, crudely cut square of cardboard would be exchanged for the price of a self-contained meal. Customers stood to wait for their order to be filled—there were no chairs or tables. These fast-food establishments were second in number only to the black-owned Southern-style diners that served full breakfasts, lunches, and dinners daily.

Mr. Hong and his family lived above his restaurant and enjoyed the advantage of being located at the busiest intersection in our mostly African American community. Across the street from King Hong Cafe, on the northwest corner of Jefferson and Market, stood People's Finance Building, one of the landmarks of Mill Creek Valley. Residents boasted about it being one of the first commercial buildings in the United States built entirely by black investors; it was the center of African American commercial, political, and social life in St. Louis. Tenants included the NAACP, the Brotherhood of Sleeping Car Porters, the Missouri Pacific and Wabash Railroad offices, and the two major black newspapers: the *St. Louis American* and the *St. Louis Argus.* There were doctors, lawyers, and insurance offices, a drug store, and a penthouse ballroom that was booked most weekends for dances and large celebrations. The Deluxe Cafe directly across Jefferson was the lunchtime place to see and be seen, a regular meeting place for business professionals and community leaders. Black politicians and some white politicians courting votes could be routinely observed eating lunch and shaking hands. The Deluxe was owned by entrepreneur Jesse Johnson, who promoted and booked nationally known black musicians. On weekends the cafe was an after-hours club where jazz musicians went to jam after their regular gigs.

Regular foot traffic at this busy crossroads provided King Hong Cafe with a steady flow of hungry patrons wanting quick and affordable lunchtime, after-school, and late-night meals. Pork and rice was popular with the teenagers that streamed from Saturday matinees at the Star and the Strand movie theaters just blocks away. A pint-size box was three-quarters filled with steamed white rice. Then slow-roasted pork shoulder, lightly seasoned with a Chinese spice blend, was diced or shredded into bite-size pieces and piled on top of the rice. Next a layer of coarsely chopped white onions was added. A final hot broth mixture of soy sauce and pork drippings (inexplicably called duck sauce) was ladled over the top. When the box was opened, the onions were steamed perfectly by the trapped temperature of the other ingredients.

Teenage boys sitting on the curb in front of "the Chinaman's" were a familiar sight. With their legs splayed and shoulders hunched, they unhooked the thin wire handle that held the folded containers together, opening the folds to create a wok-shaped paper bowl; they then tore off the flaps to mix, then scoop their portable meal into their eager mouths.

When Honey used the money he earned selling papers to buy a box of pork and rice along with his friends on the weekend, he knew it had to be eaten before he got home. Daddy didn't eat or allow Chinese food in our house because he didn't believe in "spending money on food that somebody else cooked in a restaurant with a kitchen you can't see." His main objection, as with most things, was economic, with a little culinary skepticism for good measure. To him there was no sense in paying for a box of rice for one person filled with "a lot of chopped up stuff we can't name," when there was a pot of beans or greens on the stove, seasoned with a clearly recognizable shinbone from a pig, that would feed twelve people.

Grandmama and Daddy were the only two in our family who had daily contact with white people. There was hardly ever a name used that I can recall; Grandmama would occasionally mention "my white folks" or "my white lady" when she handed over a bag of used clothing that the children in the family she worked for had outgrown. Even the children she spent her daylight hours caring for were infrequently referred to as "my chil'ren on the place." We never saw Grandmama's white folks.

Once, I begged to tag along with my grandmother and my big brother Randle on a long ride to a house that sat in the middle of a yard that looked like a park. Grandmama sat up front with Mr. Red and I sat in the back of the truck, bouncing around with Randle, who was quiet and sullen because he didn't want to be there. Mr. Red was a family friend and a sort of handyman who repaired and built things around our house that Daddy or my brothers couldn't handle. He was the only person we knew who owned his own pickup truck. When we arrived at the large yard of grass and trees, my grandmother waved at a person partially hidden behind curtains at a second-floor window. We were there to clean up all the apples that had fallen to the ground from a group of apple trees on the side of the house. Mr. Red and Randle raked large piles of rotting apples and shoveled them into burlap sacks. Grandmama and I picked up the apples that were not too bruised, and she reminded me not to pick any apples from the trees. When Grandmama walked over to talk to a person standing just inside a door on the side of the house, Randle picked two beautiful red apples from a tree, and with a grunting chuckle placed them in my bag.

When all the burlap sacks were placed along a stone wall at the front of the driveway, we got back in the truck. I looked up at the window on the second floor, then the side door, but no one was there.

My encounters with white people were incidental. There was the insurance man who came weekly to collect on the dime insurance policies that Mama had on everybody. He greeted her with a broad smile as she met him at the door with a few dollars in one hand and a stack of cardboard payment booklets in the other. The insurance man scribbled his initials in that week's box inside each folded card, collected the money, and said something about the weather and, "Thank you, Miss Ross, I'll see you next week."

There were the Glassmans at the grocery store where we "traded" every week, who Mama sometimes called "the Jews." And people on the streetcars or those working in the stores along Market Street. But they all had light skin that looked similar to Mama's and Aunt Bette's, so I was never sure if they were the white people we sometimes heard about.

———

Our hands-on, build it, make it, fix it way of life was all we knew. Imagination and ingenuity were essential qualities that children in our family and neighborhood unknowingly possessed. We used that inventiveness routinely when playing outside for hours on long summer days. My brother Honey, like all the other adolescent boys in Mill Creek, carried a stick. Not just any old crooked tree branch lying around in the alley or under a tree after a windstorm. These prized and multi-purpose spans of wood had to be the right length and heft, with the right circumference to fit snuggly in their grubby, outside-all-day-playing hands. Branches and twigs served as digging tools, pretend swords for thrusting, and make-believe rifles for shooting bad guys. A green, pliable branch with a natural curve would be notched at each end to secure a string and pulled tautly across to form a bow. Sitting cross-legged in a circle pretending to be "Indian braves," they used pocketknives, kitchen knives, and even broken soda bottles to painstakingly carve away knots and sharpen the ends of thin tree limbs into arrows for cowboy and Indian wars. Honey and his friends—Peaches, Freddy, Little Jimmy, Jerry Rigney, and Robert Roper—used their sticks to poke at rats in the ash pits, knock black walnuts out of neighbors' trees, and chase screeching cats into the tall weeds and sunflowers.

But the primary need for the stick was to ward off stray dogs. These were not pets that somehow escaped through an open door, or guard dogs that dug themselves free under fences. The alleys were the hostile territory of feral dogs that roamed among vacant lots. They knocked over garbage cans foraging for food, and deftly dodged and sprinted to evade the dogcatchers' long poles and waving nets.

Honey and the other twelve-year-old rebels could have easily played stickball in the streets or climbed trees in backyards. But the alleys had a unique allure, the attraction of an urban jungle that only boys armed with sticks understood. The long distance from most back doors to the cobbled-together fences that lined the alleys made it possible to avoid the prying eyes of adults. But the boys didn't look at each other much either. They roamed and talked and laughed, all the while looking down at the ground. They kicked clumps of dirt, rocks, and weeds along the edges of backyard fences, searching absentmindedly for nails. Every few minutes a boy would bend down, examine, and pop a nail in his pocket. Bent and even rusted nails were later straightened and cleaned up with bricks from sidewalk pavings or a crumbling ash pit wall. The ideal clay cube for pounding and hammering was a half-brick, broken to the right size for controlled striking.

Some alleys were better than others, like the alley behind Northwestern Mailbox Company on Leffingwell and Spruce Streets. It had transitioned from making simple tin mailboxes to manufacturing pinball machines years before. Most simply called it the toy factory. The loading area behind it was littered with die-cut scraps of tin in various shapes, strips of colored plastic, metal balls, springs, flippers, and plungers that could not be found anywhere else.

Other alleys yielded discarded scraps of wood: two-by-fours, one-by-twos, and one-by-sixes left over from fence or porch repairs that would become "skate trucks" outfitted with metal roller skate wheels. Or they'd become race cars made with wooden milk crates, the wheels cannibalized from abandoned baby carriages and tricycles. Randle and Honey's skate trucks and race cars were elaborately adorned with the colorful treasure from behind the toy factory, thanks to my mother's design suggestions. A two- or three-foot length of wood could be the shaft of a "top gun" to shoot soda bottle tops.

Sometimes boys lucked upon rubber inner tubes before the junkman got to them. The black rubber tubes would be cut into long thin strips with a razor blade, doubled over into a loop, and attached to one end of their sticks with a found nail. A spring clothespin affixed to the opposite end would hold the stretched, looped end of the rubber, which was then loaded with a Vess soda bottle cap in a firing position until released. Miraculously, none of the boys lost an eye, but there were plenty of cuts, scrapes, and scars for all.

Bricks were some of my favorite things. The rare unbroken rectangular building blocks were highly prized for constructing the perimeter of the playhouses I built every morning in the backyard. I swept an area of ground smooth and free of loose rocks and dirt, then stacked bricks three high at four corners, and placed a length of wood between the brick pilings to create walls for my imagined dwellings. Similarly, I made tables and benches depending on supply. Sometimes I neatly heaped dry leaves and covered the piles of leaves with sheets of newspaper, tucking the paper in around the edges to make beds for my pretend family. I adorned the open-air room with a jelly jar of yellow dandelions picked from the weeds that lined the fences. At the end of the day, I took my bricks and boards inside and stored them under my bed so that my brothers wouldn't abscond with them. My stash was safe most of the time.

The junkman was another mysterious and brave alley inhabitant. Dogs barked only briefly when his rumbling wooden pushcart passed, piled high with flattened cardboard, tin cans, and the occasional broken chair or table. He moved deliberately from trash pile to trash can. There were never any conversations between the boys and the grim-faced worker, who wore a thick brown coat and long patched pants, slick with grime, no matter the weather.

Though they kept a respectful distance and only took quick glances, there was a silent vote of admiration. It was unanimous—the junkman had the best stick of all. It was sturdy and smooth with a dark patina from years of skillful poking and prodding into the rejected rubbish of others.

Sometimes on summer afternoons, when the sun was high and hot in the sky, the boys would sit in the cool, shaded gangways between the red brick houses and rub their sticks with damp greenish-black dirt. They sat talking about comic book heroes as they mindlessly massaged the dank dirt onto the surface of their sticks. But none would admit that their diligent efforts were intended to replicate the junkman's staunch staff.

It was easy to get lost in my family of eight children, our friends, and our cousin Karen, who occasionally slept over on weekends. She willingly joined the ranks of the older girls to collectively ignore me. Karen was Aunt Bette's only child and could hardly contain her excitement about being part of our organized chaos. She meant it as a compliment when she said spending the night at our house was "like going to the circus." It wasn't lost on us that she was the only one among us who had ever actually been to a circus.

I learned the skills of finding my space in a crowd, enjoying my own thoughts, and averting my eyes to have a modicum of privacy. Temperament and personality ran the gamut in our family. Vern, the oldest, who was a popular cheerleader, swimmer, and basketball player at school, was aloof and got lost in her books at home. Randle and Beverly were the defiant ones who sneaked out at night and broke lots of rules but still managed to charm Mama. Jean had a natural maternal instinct that made her bossy, but like Honey, she was compassionate and diligent. Tootie was Daddy's favorite—he couldn't hide it, and she enjoyed it. I was a curious, outgoing, and determined child who sought attention that was in short supply: asking for what I wanted, going where I wasn't invited, and freely giving my unsolicited opinion. In other words, I was the annoying one. Ferman, the cute baby boy, joyfully accepted being adored by all.

Northern Baptist Church was where I first found the recognition and appreciation I craved. Miss Marguerite Bradley, a factory worker and part-time piano teacher, was in charge of the children at the church. She directed the junior choir and taught the young children's Sunday school class. We learned the books of the Bible, discussed how to implement the Ten Commandments in our daily lives, and recited Bible verses at her urging. We colored pictures of the fair-haired and blue-eyed Jesus depicted in the mural painted on the wall behind the pulpit and above the baptismal pool. She selected and passed out our Easter and Christmas speeches. They were printed on little slivers of paper cut from a book she purchased at the Sunday school supply store. I somehow managed to get my speeches home without losing them, and taped the pieces of paper to the wall next to my bed so that I could lie on my side with my back to the world and memorize the lines. Each year the speeches got a little longer. They were a source of anxiety until my recitation was completed in front of a larger than usual Sunday school audience that included Daddy standing in the back.

Miss Bradley taught us songs and adjusted the matching, homemade shawl collars that converted us from a Sunday school class to a junior choir on the third Sunday of each month. I was already at the church when she arrived at 10:45 a.m. on a Saturday before the third Sunday. Daddy had me come an hour early to dust the pews and windowsills before the junior choir rehearsal started. As usual, I chose large dust cloths from the box of donated clean rags made from old sheets, worn bath towels, and frayed cotton diapers. First, I'd hung one piece of cloth over the upright, back portion of a pew, letting it drape downward; then I spread a second cloth on the seat. I carefully placed my body in a seated position on top of both dust rags and scooted playfully sideways down the length of the pew. I repeated the routine, row after row, until all the varnished wood was dust-free.

When Miss Bradley entered the big double doors of the sanctuary, she predictably carried a purse in one hand and a brown envelope-style satchel filled with music books in the other. She'd walked the six blocks from the home she shared with her brother on Eugenia Street. Her head and shoulders would be folded slightly inward toward her plain white blouse in summer, the navy blue cardigan sweater that was added in fall, or a heavy brown Chesterfield coat in winter.

When she looked up to see me, her pursed brown lips broadened to a grin that seemed too big for her small, dark face. There was nothing physically attractive about Miss Bradley, but she was soft-spoken, kind, and encouraging.

After a dozen children had drifted in, she punched the piano keys with her bony fingers and directed our singing of "This Little Light of Mine" and "Yes, Jesus Loves Me" with exaggerated nods of her head. When she asked if anyone had a particular song they wanted the choir to sing, my hand flew up. I had told her earlier, before all the other kids arrived, about the songs I learned from listening to my mother's records. She played the introduction to the song we agreed on, and I burst into my best imitation of Tennessee Ernie Ford's rendition of "Old Rugged Cross." I mean, I crooned like a forty-year-old white man singing in the little whitewashed country church that was pictured on the album cover. Some of the other seven-, eight-, and nine-year-olds stared at me in disbelief; others were underwhelmed. But Miss Bradley said I did "a lovely job," and with a little more practice, she'd let me sing my song at the next Easter program.

Like Miss Bradley, Virginia Harrison was also soft-spoken, kind, and encouraging. She was on the swim team with my sister Vern, and had been voted president of their advisory class every year at Vashon High School. She and my sister Beverly were the soloists in the young adult choir at church. Ginny, as we called her, volunteered to help Miss Bradley organize the younger children for all the holiday programs. She showed us how to find our places and stand up straight. She instructed us on how to enunciate and project our voices. Where Miss Bradley was timid and plain, Ginny was poised and often described—in left-handed compliments—as "pretty for a dark-skin girl." I thought her smooth skin and slightly rounded face were beautiful, in ways that were different from my sisters. I wanted to be like her—I imitated her posture and speech—and she recognized my admiration and smiled her approval.

Ginny was the only girl among her siblings; her two older brothers were lettered athletes at Vashon. Her younger brother, who was closer to Tootie's age, was named Archie, after the professional fighter Archie Moore. The story goes that Mr. Harrison, their father, was Moore's trainer early in the fighter's long career. I never saw Mr. Harrison, but heard him described as "strict." I did see Mrs. Harrison at church occasionally when Ginny or one of her brothers escorted their mother down the center aisle of the church just before services began. She was blind and beautiful. Everything seemed to stop as she was guided to a pew toward the front of the church. To fill the silence as everyone waited for her to be seated,

Reverend Sheppard would say, in his preacher's cadence, "We are happy to see sister Lula Harrison here today," followed by a chorus of "Amen." Her complexion was noticeably fairer than her children's, who were all dark brown with sturdy builds, probably like their father. Mrs. Harrison was tall and thin with hair swept high in curls held in place by a line of small combs. She walked erect with her chin high, confident in the gentle guidance from her offspring at her elbow.

Ginny and Vern were in the 1956 graduating class at Vashon High. Vern enrolled in a postgraduate secretarial course, then later got a job in Joliet, Illinois. But Ginny was one of a few from our church who enrolled at Harris-Stowe Teachers College. She went on to earn a PhD in counseling and guidance from Saint Louis University. I'm sure Virginia Harrison was my role model when attending college became my goal.

Years later, when I was in high school, she invited me to talk to a group of eighth-grade students about what to expect when they would attend high school. I was honored. I remember that day clearly. I was speaking to the students, but I wanted to impress Ginny.

And then there was Merdean Clark. She was a few years ahead of Vern and Ginny in high school, and the most self-assured person I had ever known. Merdean had big, beautiful, almost bouffant hair and large Betty Boop eyes. Her white Peter Pan collars, unlike those worn by every young woman from sixteen to twenty-five, were more prominent and trimmed in lace or edged with ruffles. She wore bulbous clip-on earbobs that dwarfed all others. Everything she wore was just a bit more creative than everyone else. She was not soft-spoken—you knew when Merdean was in the room—but she was generous, direct, and inspiring. She once said to me, "Girl, you can sing! Now, let's get your hair together."

Merdean was a college student when she became Daddy's enthusiastic protégé in the music department at the church.

She eventually became the director of the intermediate choir. She was among the wave of young musicians and choir directors who inserted gospel music firmly amid the hymns and spirituals sung during Sunday morning worship.

Merdean's bold and stylish way of being herself influenced my approach to all things creative, and gave me permission to be comfortable with my own ideas—all I needed was a nudge toward the light.

———————

I didn't really need to look very far for my light. Everybody said Jean was the prettiest of the Ross girls. She looked most like the pictures of Mama when Mama was young. Their resemblance was especially striking when we looked back at the few surviving photographs from Mama's childhood and college days. Both had long, lean bodies, lots of thick hair, and the same barely smiling expressions. Not one youthful picture exists of Carol Jean Ross with a toothy grin. Probably because she was impatiently waiting to get the picture-taking done so that she could move on to the next thing.

Also like Mama, Jean was an organizer. She would hold the kickball until all the rules were made and she had double-checked to be sure that the teams were even. She was always the first to get dressed and finish her chores on Saturday mornings. Because we had to go everywhere in pairs or groups, she would be annoyed if anyone made her wait. She was not a follower and was very comfortable with being in charge.

Mama assigned the four older children to oversee the four younger children on school days. That meant they made sure we got up and dressed, had breakfast, packed our lunches, and got off to school. Jean was responsible for me, and she took her role seriously. She combed and braided my hair before bed, then brushed the edges of my hairline with an extra application of

Dixie Peach pomade every morning. Her unconscious preening continued as she rubbed the thick residue of oil that was left on her hands onto my ashy face and scuffed knees.

She would silently strip the threadbare sheets from my bed when they were wet and put them in the washing machine for Mama to wash. On the mornings when my sheets were dry, she grabbed my hands, found her elusive smile, and we did a bedside happy dance. Mama handed out milk money, signed report cards or permission slips, and did a final check as we filed past her bedroom door to leave for school. Jean proudly presented *me* for approval.

In June of 1957, Lincoln School closed its hundred-year-old doors forever. Just about every child that lived in the formerly stately Victorian homes, shabby row houses, or more dilapidated rooming houses from Bernard Street to Locust and from Leffingwell to Twentieth Street had started their elementary education there. Mama said people were moving west and there were not enough kids to keep the school open. Some kids transferred to nearby Johnson School, others had to trek all the way to Compton and Market to Waring School. Ferman and I would be walking across the Jefferson Bridge with the big kids starting in September.

But there were too many kids for the old Attucks School on Papin also. Two branch schools constructed of corrugated metal were built to accommodate the additional students from the near north side of the railroad tracks. Our school was located two blocks east on Chouteau and Twenty-Third Street. The single-story building had one long central "shotgun" corridor from the front door to the back door, which led out to the asphalt-covered schoolyard. There were four bright classrooms on each side of the hallway for children in kindergarten through the third grade. Jean walked the two long blocks past her school every morning to drop Ferman and me off at "Branch No. 1," and was there waiting for us in the afternoon when school let out.

Jean made it her business to know where I was and what I was doing for the first ten years of my life. When I thought I had learned all she had to teach, I arrogantly pulled away. She watchfully stepped aside, but never too far. Even as a teenager, she was always ready to teach me a life lesson in a wry, matter-of-fact tone that also seemed to mimic Mama.

There was a repurposed Crisco shortening can covered with a saucer that sat on the back of our kitchen stove as a receptacle for "bacon drippings," generally known as "grease," or what Daddy called "the po' man's butter." We used the sweet, smoky elixir to fry everything from fish on Fridays to baloney and fried eggs for sandwiches on Saturday afternoons, or crispy chicken and fried green tomatoes on Sundays. On cool fall and winter days, the liquid grease solidified, the heavier flecks separated and fell to the bottom of the can, and a smooth off-white grease rose to the top like cream. When I thought no one was looking, I took a finger full of what seemed to me a reasonable substitute for Vaseline and smeared it on my perpetually scuffed and dry knees and legs. While reveling in my resourcefulness, I heard a familiar voice over my shoulder. It was Jean. In a remarkably non-judgmental voice she said, "That's why dogs and cats are always following you. You smell like bacon."

There were a lot of kids in our house, but not as many as the Lattimores. There were twelve of them, one matched to each of us plus four much older to spare. There were Lattimore and Ross children in just about every grade at Lincoln, and later, Attucks schools. And they had cool nicknames too: Chink, Litt, Sook, Bull, Cat, Papa, and Butch. The youngest girl, Jackie (her family called her Jack), was my best friend; she always had a big thumb-sucker's grin and a happy, raspy laugh. We played house and school all summer long in each other's backyards—me with bare feet because my school shoes had worn out by then. We brushed and braided each other's hair when we played beauty salon. Her hair was longer and softer than mine. She had bangs that I rolled, and tucked, and patted, and smoothed for as long as she'd allow.

Ferman and Butch rode broomsticks for horses while shooting each other with their pointed fingers and sounds of *pop*, *pow*, and *ping*. Papa was an amateur bantamweight boxer and walked Tootie home from school before going to the gym. Clinton, who didn't have a nickname, was in Honey's class, but had a crush on my sister Jean, who was a grade ahead of him. She didn't know he was alive. Beverly and Bull were boyfriend and girlfriend. Beverly sneaked out to see him after Mama and Daddy were asleep. She had to climb out and back in the middle-room window because the back door creaked and needed a hefty shove to open and close.

The Lattimores lived one street over on Randolph. We would cut through the gangway alongside Mr. St. Clair's store to get to each other's houses. Their house was much better than our dimly lit, crowded three rooms of beds and chifforobes. Theirs was a big two-family flat with a fenced-in side yard. The older children slept in the second-floor apartment. We weren't allowed to go inside of anyone's house, which made me more curious about how other people lived. I peeked inside the kitchen when Jackie and I played school on her back porch. Sometimes I went to the front door looking for Jackie, but I never went beyond their front hall. I would look into the living room that was off to the side. It was bright and neat—like a display room; everyone walked past it to get to the bedrooms and kitchen. No one ever sat on the maroon velveteen sofa. I loved looking at their living room. We didn't have a living room or a sofa.

Mrs. Lattimore was friendly; she and Jackie had the same joyous laugh. Mr. Lattimore was the rare black man who had a "good job" as a supervisor at Laclede Gas Company. Like Daddy, he probably missed serving in World War II because of the married-man-with-dependents deferment, and as a result, advanced in his position during the war years. He also stood out when he got a shiny new Buick every other year. Mysterious, stern, and a little scary, his "lazy eye" marked all the Lattimore boys. He didn't smile and never called his children by their names; it was "Come here, boy," or "Come here, girl." They always knew which of them he was talking to. His car pulled up in front of the Lattimore house every evening around six o'clock. Mrs. Lattimore had his dinner ready. All was quiet in the Lattimore house as he ate his meal and read the evening newspaper. Mr. Lattimore's car in front of their house was everyone's signal to be someplace else.

———————

The city landscape of my childhood was made up of some conspicuous components with important and varied functions. Gangways were the narrow spaces between two buildings that made it possible to access rear entrances and provided shortcuts to alleys and adjacent streets. Our block between Jefferson and Leffingwell was a long walk around if we wanted to get to Mr. Emmet's store on Spruce to buy orange frappé or to play with Jackie Lattimore. In the mornings, adults headed to work at factories and small businesses scattered throughout the neighborhood, joining children who cut through gangways and alleys to get to school. During the heat of summer days, they were a cool retreat from the sun. At sundown, they were equally important to children playing hide and seek as they were to petty criminals fleeing the scene of a crime. Even later in the evening, they were convenient lovers' lanes.

At the rear of the gangways were paths flanked by extended narrow backyards dotted with weathered wooden outhouses. When my grandmother bought our house in 1950, its best feature was the jerry-rigged toilet in the hall beneath the second-floor landing and next to the door leading to the basement. A cold-water sink was later squeezed into the small space that required us to turn sideways to get past it. But there were plenty of landlords who were not willing to go to the expense of installing additional indoor plumbing for renters.

Mr. and Mrs. Sinclair, who owned the candy store across from our house, had the ultimate poor man's status symbol: an outhouse with a three-foot high brick wall base topped with painted wood and a shingled roof. Mrs. Sinclair was an obese woman with a pretty face that looked like a plump peach. She scooted around behind the counter on a stool outfitted with wheels to retrieve canned goods, loaves of bread, ice cream, and candy for her customers. When she needed to be indisposed, she locked the cash register and put a sign up in the window near the door that read: *Back in 15 Minutes.* Everyone knew she was headed for the only outhouse in the neighborhood that could accommodate her rotund form. She was confident that old Mr. Trotter, who sat on his front porch all day, was watching, and would ward off anyone attempting to enter the unlocked store.

But marauding boys knew that if Mr. Trotter was not on his porch, and the sign was in the window, that was their chance to reach around the end of the display counter and get a handful of penny candy or bags of potato chips clipped to a wire stand. Contraband in hand, they would dash laughing for a nearby gangway or, even better, to the field of sunflowers that shot skyward every summer on the vacant lot at the end of our block. The same boys who were cunning enough to risk a whooping for stealing candy were daring enough to challenge each other in pretend sword fights and spear-thrusting battles with the long prickly stalks of the sunflowers. The sting of the thorny spines was just dangerous enough to inflict welts and scratches that belied the beauty of the flowers. The boys dared each other to run the gauntlet through the giant maze of green and yellow and come out on the other side victorious.

Randle was the family tough guy with a soft center. He walked in front of all the other boys to play a game of stickball that involved hitting a hurled craggy black walnut with a broom handle. He was the first to throw a punch in a fistfight with rivals from another block. Skirting danger in a tire-rolling race, with Honey tucked inside the opening where a car wheel would be, he pulled the lumbering tire to a sliding stop just short of oncoming traffic. Randle was the strong big brother who lifted Ferman and me from the floor by our belts like human barbells to build his muscles, then entertained us by blowing smoke rings from the cigarettes he bummed off other boys, or telling scary stories at bedtime. He was quick to share anything he pilfered from the Jewish stores and fruit stands along Market Street while Mama, unaware of his mischief, haggled and bargained for the best deals.

Attracted to dangerous fun, he and his friends used BB guns to shoot rats in the basement. They tied a long string to the pull chain on the light socket hanging from the ceiling and put a cracker smeared with peanut butter on top of a crumpled newspaper that was placed in the middle of the floor as bait. When all the boys were seated or squatting in positions high off the floor, one boy pulled the chain to turn off the single light bulb. Then they all sat, waiting in the dark without talking. They knew the routine: be still, listen for the soft sound of the newspaper rustling, the cracker crumbling, and the rats squeaking. After minutes of tense waiting, Randle barked, "Now!" The light bulb snatched on, the sound of compressed air pellet fire, the crack and ding and thud of BBs striking, and the whooping, yelling, laughing, and rats darting was all over in seconds. The loud hand slapping, jumping, and exaggerated recounting went on for another ten minutes. There was never a dead rat to show for their military-style ambushes—a fact that was lost in their excitement. They filed out of the basement to the street, sat on the curb under the streetlight, and replayed the adventure again and again.

Fiercely protective of his family, Randle was ready to defend his sisters and mother from the slightest threat or insult. One summer evening a friend came running toward him, yelling that our mother had been robbed. He raced a block to find her on the ground, colorless, with a scraped elbow and knee. Urgently pushing others aside, he knelt beside her. "Mama, are you alright? What happened?"

She described how three boys she didn't know came up behind her and said, "Hey, white lady, what you doing around here? I fell against the building and then to one knee when they shoved me and snatched my purse." She had walked the blocks along Leffingwell from her church on Washington Avenue many times, it was not dark, she knew everyone, and she felt safe.

The news reached the rest of us: "Your mother's hurt." "Yo' mama's been robbed." "Miss Frances is on the ground beside Mr. Cotton's store." Beverly, the fastest runner of the girls, arrived next, then Jean and me, each with a single refrain: "Mama!" "Mama!" "Mama!"

She sat on the ground with her back to the brick wall and her long legs to the side with her dress smoothed to cover her scraped knee. She was not the willowy athletic college dropout that arrived in St. Louis anymore. Nearly twenty years later, she had had eight children and by her own calculation, had gained ten pounds with each. She sat on the ground and looked up at a cocoon of concerned brown faces while she took the time she needed to regain her composure and the will to get to her feet. Then Randle and Beverly helped her up and slowly walked her the remaining half-block home.

Delivered safely to her bed, my mother—her wounds already turning red and purple—was tended by my sisters. Randle turned and ran back to the scene of the crime. Neighbors who had witnessed the assault provided information about who the offenders might be and pointed him in the direction they had run. Randle found Mama's purse and its contents in a nearby alley. He gathered her belongings and took them back home to her. The coin purse was empty of the few dollars she carried, but she was relieved to find the plastic sleeves that held her social security card, NAACP membership, and her children's library cards.

Mama knew that Randle would seek revenge, so in her most calming voice she pleaded, "I'm not hurt, baby—so leave it alone." We all knew that would not be the case. A few days later Randle fought with one of the boys he accused of robbing Mama. When the fight was over, and Randle and his friends were walking away, someone jumped on Randle's back and violently bit off the top of his right ear. Randle came home with his bloody shirt balled up and covering his ear. Mama pulled the shirt away and asked, "What happened?" as she inspected the bite-shaped gap in the top of his ear. He matter-of-factly told the story that led to the fight and bite, and Mama listened as she washed and applied Mercurochrome to the side of his face. She cut the bottom off of one of Daddy's Sunday undershirts and wrapped it as a bandage over his ear and around his head. With the wound cleaned and covered, Mama asked, "Where is the part that was bitten off?" Randle hunched his shoulders and said, "I don't know, I guess it's up the street on the ground somewhere." Mama said, "Well, you and Honey go back up there and find it. We'll take it to the hospital and see if they can sew it back on." They did, but the doctors couldn't or wouldn't reattach it, so just like that, Randle had another war wound, even better than the long scar over his left eye, to prove his toughness.

Randle was tall like Mama. One day Daddy and Randle stood in the small front hallway with their heaving chests almost touching. Daddy peered up at him angrily, keeping his head level. Mama shooed Tootie and me back into the middle room. We heard Daddy's raised voice, then tussling and shuffling sounds, and then Mama screamed, "No!" The screen door slammed. I ran to see what was happening, but could only see the bottom of Daddy's shoes and his lower legs lying on the floor before Tootie pulled me back. Randle had been barreling toward this moment maybe all of his life.

Mama had gotten a phone call from Randle's school earlier that day—just weeks before his high school graduation. He'd been involved in an altercation which resulted in a female student bystander falling down a flight of stairs. He was expelled and could not attend his graduation ceremony. When Daddy got home, his disappointment and frustration escalated to the physical. Randle said later that Daddy lost his balance and fell backward onto his injury-shortened leg when Randle tried to fend off an oncoming strike from Daddy's raised hand. But the unthinkable was done.

A few days later, Randle and Mama went to the recruitment office downtown. He scored well on the Armed Services Vocational Aptitude Battery and enlisted in the Marine Corps.

FIVE

The year 1958 was pivotal for the Ross family. Daddy got a financial settlement from his accident and was enjoying his a new, better paying job as a truck driver. Randle became a leatherneck. And Sam, the first grandchild, was born on Valentine's Day. He was a surprise to me; I thought the baggy shirts Beverly wore were her quirky new fashion statement. LaVerne moved to Joliet, Illinois, to live with her godmother, and got an office job at the state prison there. Daddy got our first and only new car, a beautiful sky-blue 1957 Ford station wagon, the one with the big round taillight.

And then in late October we moved to an eight-room house in the Hamilton Heights neighborhood. The house had hot water from the faucets, a furnace with radiators in every room, and a built-in white porcelain tub with a shower. We were in heaven. Our front and back yards were called lawns—with grass. There was furniture, too: a beautiful mahogany dining room set, a sleek dusty-rose living room sofa and chair set, even new beds in all the bedrooms. Jean and Tootie shared an attic room that was big enough for them to divide into individual spaces of their own. I'm not sure that we even used a truck to move, because there was nothing worth taking from our old house in Mill Creek but our clothes, quilts, Mama's business and sewing boxes, and a few pots and pans.

I won't forget turning the corner onto Oakley Place, riding in the back seat of our new car. Looking past my parents' shoulders and through the front windshield, I saw a taupe and pale-green tunnel made of trees that lined both sides of our new street. Mama read my mind and said, "Those are sycamore trees." I had never seen trees in those colors before. The October sunlight that sparkled through the fluttering leaves was like a dream I'd never had.

Our new school was only two blocks away and looked like a beautiful brick-and-stone castle that took up the whole block of Minerva Street between Hamilton and Goodfellow Avenues. The front entrance sat at the top of three sets of wide stone steps, separated by two broad landings; in front of it, a terraced lawn with a line of trees stretched from one end of the building to the next. The tall front windows were stained glass at the top, like a church, but with scenes of children frolicking instead of Jesus at the Last Supper.

It was October when we transferred to Hempstead School, and we had missed the first important weeks. Everybody had chosen their friends already, and none of the kids in my class lived on my block. But it didn't take long for me to make new friends. And I soon learned one of the cardinal rules of fourth grade: the first one to miss a word during the weekly spelling bee will get teased at recess. Well, no one knew that rule better than me. If I had spent as much time studying my spelling words as I did praying—"Lord, please, just don't let me be the first to miss a word"—I would have gotten well beyond the first round. I didn't mind being the second to sit. If somehow I got to the third round, it was as glorious as winning for me. I had no delusions about being the last kid standing. I just wanted to get lost in the middle and escape shame for another week.

I wasn't good at spelling, and I was a really slow reader. I made low murmuring sounds during silent reading times that annoyed the students next to me. I had to decide whether to sound out the words softly to myself or silently look at the words over and over while I got further and further behind the other kids. I hardly ever finished my reading assignment before we moved on to something else.

I never volunteered to go to the blackboard, even if I thought I knew the answer. I couldn't take the chance that a teacher might ask a follow-up question that would expose me to humiliation. I spent a lot of time thinking about how to hide my reading problems. When the teacher had each student read parts of a chapter aloud in class, I would count row by row, desk by desk, to figure out which paragraphs I might likely have to read. Then I practiced them while the other kids were reading their passages. I even took into account that some sections were shorter than others and the teacher might have a student read two. I was so distracted by the counting and practicing that I rarely heard what the other kids were saying. Consequently, at the end of class, my paragraphs were just a jumbled group of words with no relationship to the lessons. Much of school was a secret game in which I tried to stay two or three moves ahead with the single goal of avoiding embarrassment.

Shame was a powerful motivator. The threat of humiliation spurred me to read whenever and whatever I could outside of school. We didn't have a lot of books in our home, but I read my brothers' comics and my mother's *McCall's* magazines. Mama subscribed to *Highlights* children's magazine, which had lots of pictures and games. But my favorite was the incomplete set of used *Childcraft* encyclopedias (the C and W volumes were missing) that Daddy had brought home one day in a heavy cardboard box. I read about people, places, and things at my own slow pace, and my teacher told Mama that I often had "far more background knowledge than the other kids during class discussions." I didn't know what that meant, but it seemed to please Mama.

I wanted to read about the beautiful trees with a funny name. When I asked Mama how to spell sycamore, she slowly pronounced the syllables—"syc-a-more"—and spelled

"S-Y-C-A-M-O-R-E. "Sometimes Y sounds like an I," she explained. Sycamore with a *y*: another spelling rule was locked into my memory bank. The trees became one of my favorite things about our new home. They touched above our narrow street to create a tall leafy canopy. At certain times of the year, the bark peeled off in large curved sheets that crackled loudly when I broke them or stepped on them. In the fall, when the large, dry, brown leaves fell, Ferman and I raked them high, then jumped from the front porch and rolled around in them until the crunching sound stopped and our hair and clothes were covered with fine brown confetti.

We saw little white faces peering out at us from the windows next door. We sometimes heard children playing in the backyard in the early morning or after school, but when we came outside, they ran inside. By November, when it started to get dark earlier, we didn't see or hear them anymore.

Most of the white families had moved from our new neighborhood of short, curving streets, hidden near the westernmost city limits, a few years before our family's arrival. But there were several white families still living on our block when we moved in that fall. They may have been reluctant to leave this charming enclave of boxy, sandstone houses with terra-cotta shingled roofs that the real estate agent told Mama were built by German immigrants in the 1920s. But by the following spring, there was only one white family left in the entire neighborhood. Mr. and Mrs. Russell lived with their grandson, Butch, in a pristine white house on a double lot next to the corner grocery store. They erected an ugly chain link fence around their beautiful manicured yard—it might as well have been a "KEEP OUT" sign. Mama said she never even saw moving trucks when the white families left.

Mr. Turner was the first to integrate the neighborhood in 1953. He was already a white-haired, retired widower with no children when we met him. He had a farm in Lebanon,

Illinois, that had been in his family since they left Mississippi in 1910. He generously distributed fresh fruits and vegetables to his neighbors from the wraparound porch of his white corner house and occasionally took some of the boys fishing. He and his wife had lived on Lawton Street in Mill Creek when he returned from France at the end of World War I.

The newly arriving black families tended to be younger than ours and were an impressive community of educators, nurses, small business owners, and postal and auto workers who started moving in as early as 1956. Mr. Mershon around the corner and Mrs. Goble across the street were high school teachers. Mr. Goble was a supervisor at General Cable Corporation; he worked there from the time he graduated from Lincoln University until the company closed in 1980. Mr. and Mrs. Dupree next door owned several small businesses. One of the city's few African American judges, Clyde Cahill, and his family lived three houses over on our short street of only twelve houses. All the families had young children, so my sisters and I were in high demand as babysitters.

Our house, and especially the large front porch, quickly became a hub of neighborhood activity. Music streamed through the open doors and windows, the smell of fresh popcorn wafted, and sweet red Kool-Aid flowed. One summer evening, we lost track of time, and Daddy suddenly appeared on the sidewalk under the huge sycamore tree in front of our house. Kids parted like the Red Sea and teenage boys sheepishly hunched their shoulders and lowered their chins, backing away and mumbling, "Hi, Mr. Ross." Daddy walked up the steps to the front porch with the slight limp that rocked him heavily from side to side, a result of the accident that both crushed his left leg and bankrolled our improved living conditions. As he crossed the porch, he paused, and with one sweeping motion of his head, made eye contact with his children. He said in a low, stern voice that was only heard by us, "Turn that music down. No wonder white folks don't want to be bothered with y'all. Get in this house." I fell in line with my sisters as we followed Daddy inside, but I couldn't help but wonder: What white folks?

As the older kids became teens and got as tall as Daddy, the whooping lineups ended. But there was one last beating that will always be seared in my memory. It was shortly after we moved, but Jean had opted to finish high school near Mill Creek, at Hadley Tech on Grand and Bell.

One summer evening in 1959, Jean and a few friends went skating at the outdoor Steinberg Skating Rink in Forest Park. They knew their curfew and left the rink in time to catch the two buses to get home before Daddy locked the front door. All the other kids went as a group, but Jean lagged behind with her boyfriend, Sharron Washington, who was the star quarterback for the Hadley High School football team. Just as they were coming out of the park, the northbound bus pulled away. After eight in the evening, the buses ran only once an hour. So they started walking the ten blocks toward Page Avenue, where she would catch the Page-Wellston bus, and Sharron would walk a few blocks east to where he lived near Taylor Avenue.

When she got off the bus at Hamilton and Page, Mama and Tootie were waiting at the bus stop. It was after eleven. Mama asked calmly, "Where have you been?" Jean explained that she and Sharron had missed the first bus and had to walk to Page. Mama took in a long deep breath, released it, and stated, "You know Daddy's gonna whoop you." Jean said, "Yes, ma'am." They walked home without talking.

Mama went inside the house first and talked to Daddy, who was sitting in the living room. Jean went to the third floor, where she shared a room with Tootie. A few minutes later, Daddy called up the stairs, "Git down here." Already changed into her pajamas, Jean walked down the stairs like she was going to the gallows. When she stepped through the door from the third floor, he began beating her like I had never seen him beat any of us. She crumpled to the floor, covered her head and screamed with every strike. After what seemed like long minutes of a powerful assault on Jean's small pale body—it was probably no more than thirty seconds—Mama said, "ENOUGH." Daddy stopped his arm and the belt in midair; sweating, he turned and walked away.

I hated Daddy for the first time that night. When the crying and sniffing quieted, I went to the kitchen, got a butcher's knife, and put it under my pillow intending to kill him during the night—something I had probably seen in an *Alfred Hitchcock Presents* or *Twilight Zone* episode on television.

I slept through the night, and the next morning the knife was still under my pillow. Daddy had already left for church, but Jean was nowhere to be found. We searched the house from top to bottom, the yard, the neighborhood. Then we searched again. Our basement had a walk-in iron vault that had a heavy bolt that Daddy locked in the engaged position to prevent it from completely closing. Inside the vault was a large cedar chest filled with quilts and winter coats. Tootie and I twice struggled to lift the lid, then stood on tiptoes to look into the deep chest. On the third time, Jean uncovered her head. She looked like a wild woman. Her eyes were red and puffy from crying, and her hair was sticking out in all directions. We all started crying; I didn't know whether to be happy that she hadn't run away, or sad that she was so beaten up. Her arms, legs, and back were striped with red outlines from Daddy's belt.

She wanted something to drink, so we brought her milk. Later, we brought her Kool-Aid and sandwiches. Then, we brought her clothes. We were prepared to hide her in the basement for the rest of her life. But Mama must have noticed our coming and going, and the next thing we knew she was standing at the door.

We helped Jean out of the chest and took her to Mama's bed. We put salve on her welts, cold towels on her eyes, and brushed her hair.

We never talked about that night again.

By February of 1959, the demolition of buildings in Mill Creek Valley had already begun, to make way for the new Daniel Boone Expressway planned to go through the heart of downtown St. Louis. But the plume of dust from crumbling concrete and Missouri's finest red clay bricks was still some distance away from the 2600 block of Bernard Street. Most of the houses between Jefferson and Leffingwell were empty. There was no more Sinclair's Candy Store or Miss Marguerite's Beauty Shop. Nor was there competition for the coveted spot on the street where Mr. Thigpen parked his prized 1952 Mercury sedan.

Mercy Seat Baptist Church had anchored the west end of our street for many years but was now empty. The congregation had marched twenty blocks in a jubilant parade to their new church on Washington Avenue between Newstead and Boyle. Our church, Northern Baptist, had moved too, more than thirty blocks west from the location on Ewing Avenue to the corner of Maple and Belt. It replaced the former Maple Avenue Methodist Episcopal Church, which had moved its dwindling white congregation to St. Louis County. The distance from Ewing was too far for us to parade to our new location, so church members gathered in their Sunday best, some in their ushers' uniforms and others in billowing choir robes, at the intersection of Delmar and Belt. Then we marched and sang the four remaining blocks north that led us to the beautiful white stone edifice. Our new church, which took up a half block, had high, arched wood-paneled doors and large round stained glass windows on two sides. The church members were so proud of our new home, but Honey saw it as three times more church for us to dust and clean every Saturday.

Our family had moved from the old neighborhood almost six months before, in the fall of 1958. Grandmama, as the owner of our old house, received payment for its sale and a one hundred dollar relocation allotment from the city. It was enough to put a down payment on a small two-family house of her own. Her new home was near a bus line that cut her travel time to work in half. She got a "good deal" on a house that had been damaged in a tornado that sliced through midtown St. Louis in February of 1959. What had been the kitchen of the house was blown away, leaving only the stone foundation that became a large back porch on the shortened house. She rented out the second floor to help pay the mortgage.

Back on Bernard Street, Saturdays were teeming with other fleeing residents who used cars, pickup trucks, and moving vans to load furniture, boxes, and appliances. Starting early each Monday morning and throughout the weekdays, a convoy of trucks crewed by scavenging white men roamed the streets. The men loaded these trucks with abandoned cast iron stoves and door frames with the doors and transoms still attached. They carefully removed stained glass windows, ornate wood trim, and pews from unoccupied churches. Days after Mr. Cotton moved his ice cream and candy store to a different (and according to Daddy, smaller) location on Vandeventer near St. Louis Avenue, looters removed the sizable mounted mirror that stretched high and wide behind his counter.

But the century-old bricks from the crumbling neighborhood were the most profitable. Teams of men with picks and hammers knocked down houses before the wrecking balls arrived; they piled bricks on wooden pallets and hauled them away on flatbed trucks. The lowly junkmen and ragmen who used to be relegated to the alleys now pushed their overloaded carts along the streets, stopped them at the curb, and freely walked in and out of the empty houses, salvaging what they could carry.

Some people stayed behind longer than others, like the Hornes on Garrison Street. They owned their house and were reluctant to leave. In her book *Mother's Wit,* Malaika Horne writes warmly about her family's life in Mill Creek. They lived only a few blocks from our house on Bernard, but I don't remember them. Though we were close in age, they went to a different school, and a few blocks were practically a different neighborhood for children. Churches drew their congregations from the broader community, but she wrote that her mother didn't attend church because "she didn't have the clothes," nor could she afford to have her hair "fixed." But Mrs. Horne dressed her three younger children in their "Sunday best," gave them nickels for an offering, and "trotted" them off to Northern Baptist Church—*our church.* When Malaika described the church as "the pride of the worshipers, it was immaculately kept with shiny wooden pews," I yelled into the pages of the opened book with unbridled pride: "We cleaned that church!"

In 2015 I met Gwen [Horne] Moore (the middle sister of the Horne siblings) while doing research at the Missouri History Museum. She was curating a major exhibit for the museum on the history of civil rights in St. Louis, called: *#1 in Civil Rights.* Gwen's "recollection," as captured in her sister's book, regarding those last days in Mill Creek was poignant: "I don't know if there was collective resistance to this 'Negro removal,' but it seems to me that the most affected people had the least amount to say about their destinies." Gwen added, "My parents held out for as long as they could, until 1960. They were trying to get a decent price for the property they had worked so hard and sacrificed so much to acquire. We were the last to leave on our block."

My sister Tootie's friend Plum, whose family had lived across from us on Bernard Street, was still there when Grandmama finally moved away. But we saw her, her mother, and grandmother at church every Sunday. On Sundays, she huddled happily with Tootie in the back of the Sunday school classroom to talk about school friends and how things were changing on the block. She and Tootie had finished seventh grade together and would have been walking to school on the first day if we had not moved. Instead, Plum descended the stairs that led from her rear-entry second-floor apartment and waved to old Mr. Trotter who was at his usual post on his front porch. His daughter Leola and her son, Clem, had moved away. Now there was only him, his second adult daughter, Molly, and Mrs. Trotter, whom we had not seen outside the house for years.

When Plum turned south at the end of the block, the Jefferson Bridge stretched before her in the distance with cars and trucks straddling streetcar tracks in both directions—but no other children were walking to school. She was the very last child on our street to attend Attucks School. Everyone on our street had called her Plum, but her teachers called her Eleanor. All the kids in her class now lived on the south side of Chouteau and nobody called her Plum anymore.

The school had been at the same location near the Jefferson Bridge on Papin Street since the late 1800s. It was first called Chouteau School after one of the founding families of St. Louis, who owned much of the land through which the long-ago drained creek had flowed. As the more affluent city residents moved west and the population shifted, it was renamed Colored School No. 4, and then renamed again for Crispus Attucks, the black man purported to be the first American patriot killed in the Revolutionary War.

Plum told Tootie about how she roamed among the empty houses after school, homes her mother didn't allow her to visit when they were occupied—including ours. The house we left behind was strewn with a jumble of old bunk beds and dressers that were too shabby to take to our new home. The only bed we moved was Mama's. We left the chifforobes because the new house had closets in every bedroom, and the flimsy curtains still hung at the windows in the front room. Daddy had removed the door from our old refrigerator with the broken handle so that no one could get trapped inside.

In their Sunday chats, Plum confessed to once having a favorite spot for sitting in her front room where she looked onto Bernard Street and at our front yard directly across the street. That vantage point provided a clear view and reliable entertainment for Plum on countless late afternoons when she was home alone after school. She used to watch silently as neighborhood children romped and played on the street below. Sometimes she broke her mother's rule and let Tootie and me come upstairs and eat a snack with her. She had a room of her own that was just big enough for her twin bed and a chest of drawers—there was no window. She had an oscillating fan on the chest in summer, but slept with the door to her room open in winter to warm it from the freestanding gas heater in her mother's bedroom. Tootie and I envied Plum's neat bedroom that she didn't have to share with anyone as much as Plum craved our raucous, laughing brood of eight children with a mother and "real" father. She described how she watched and listened as we played outside in summer from morning until the streetlights came on at dusk. She watched as Mama sat just inside our gate, crocheting and chatting with passersby, and as Daddy came home from one job and left for another. Plum knew us all by name and sight and said she wondered about what we did inside our house when all was finally quiet outside.

After a few months in our new neighborhood, which was so different from the old one that it seemed to me like it was from a storybook, we reconnected with some of our former neighbors. It turned out that realtors had steered many of us to the same general location in the northwest end of the city. The Lattimores moved to the 5600 block of Maple, which was on the walking route we took to church. I stopped to visit almost every Sunday after church to talk to my friend Jackie and Mrs. Lattimore. Mr. Trotter resumed his porch-sitting at his new two-family house on Hamilton near Wells Avenue. I waved to him on Saturday afternoons when I walked to shop at the J. C. Penney store on Easton Avenue in the Wellston shopping district—but I'm not sure that he knew it was me.

Tootie and Plum were eventually classmates again at Soldan High School on Union Boulevard.

We loved our new home and neighborhood, but there was such a stark difference in where and how we had lived before in Mill Creek—it confused me. If we could have lived in a clean, spacious house with modern amenities before, why didn't we? I wondered, but I didn't ask my parents why. I just enjoyed our new life. The first years were wonderful; having hot water for washing dishes and bathing was the best. I still shared a room with my younger brother, but I had a bed of my own for the first time. Daddy's complaints about waste now extended to the overuse of hot water and lights. If he heard the shower running longer than he thought it should, he'd bang on the bathroom door and yell, "It doesn't take *that* long to clean your body—turn that hot water off!" If it wasn't the excessive consumption of hot water, it was the unnecessary use of electricity—mainly leaving lights on in empty rooms. By Daddy's calculation, three times the additional living space had resulted in ten times the cost of utilities. And it was his responsibility to monitor and conserve: "Why do you need two lamps on to read a book?" "Who left that light on in the kitchen?" "You don't need a light on to watch television."

All the homes in Hamilton Heights had beautiful fireplaces in the living rooms. Most had decorative screens and grates with artificial logs. Halfway through the first winter of buying fuel for our oil furnace, Daddy dumped a pile of wood at the back end of our driveway. We were chopping and stacking firewood again and were the only family in the entire neighborhood that used our fireplace to heat our home.

As I got older, I began to understand more of my parents' conversations about the changes in our new neighborhood. The blatant segregation and benign neglect that plagued our old community they now referred to with new terms: "redlining" and "white flight."

Many of the families with children from Mill Creek moved to the newly built, federally funded, public high-rise Pruitt-Igoe Projects. If Daddy had not received his moderate financial settlement, we, no doubt, would have been moved to Pruitt-Igoe as well.

My parents said that the white people who lived in the lovely homes in that far west end of the city, north of Delmar Boulevard, had been "sacrificed." Realtors, politicians, and insurance companies had worked together to implement a housing plan without regard for the civil rights or social norms of all involved—black or white. It was a forgone conclusion that when a few black families moved in, the white people would flee, thereby creating space for the displaced. In short order, we were in a segregated community again. As if with a touch of a magic wand, Soldan High School became a black school, and white churches continued their pilgrimages further west. St. Paul African Methodist Episcopal Church had recently relocated a block from our house at the corner of Hamilton and Julian. It had been on an early list of several historic churches that would remain standing in Mill Creek. But in the end, only one small black church that was supported by white Episcopalians survived.

It wasn't long before the quaint bakery with freshly baked bread, pastries, and doughnuts closed. Then the well-stocked corner drug store was replaced with a liquor store. Bookmobiles parked at designated intersections every other Saturday to replace the small branch library that closed at the corner of Hamilton and Eastern Ave (now Martin Luther King Boulevard). Joe's Record Store, which replaced the library, streamed soulful music from outdoor speakers. A laundromat replaced the dry cleaner, and there was no longer a shoe repair shop nearby. Bill Kohn, the Jewish man who owned and operated the corner grocery, held on the longest. National Food Store, the supermarket a few blocks away on Hodiamont Avenue closed, and the building became a community social services and job training center. The nearest discount supermarket was a bus ride away.

There were so many families with kids in the handsome four- and six-family apartment buildings east of our street that the schools quickly became overcrowded. First, they built classroom modules in the schoolyard. By 1961, Ferman and I were bused back downtown to separate schools in Mill Creek, which by then, thanks to its bombed-out landscape, was being called "Hiroshima Flats." Our school bus passed acres of desolate wasteland with a few new high-rise buildings jutting upward on the border of St. Louis University. I attended sixth- and seventh-grade classes in the basement of Vashon High School, which had an unobstructed view of the empty space where my family and friends had lived a few years before. My younger brother and I continued to be bused to separate schools for the remainder of our elementary education. I graduated from eighth grade at Clinton Elementary School with poor white children who had not yet fled downtown's near south-side Clinton-Peabody public housing project. In keeping with the St. Louis tradition of segregation, Clinton-Peabody had been built for indigent whites on the south side of downtown in 1947, at the same time that Carr-Square Village was built a few miles across Fourteenth Street for blacks on the near north side.

The patterns were repeating; too many underemployed black people were being herded into a designated confined area. Many had never owned or maintained homes before, and like us, could scarcely afford to heat them in winter. White flight and disinvestment, followed by an influx of illegal drugs in the seventies, overwhelmed the community. The departure of the black middle class was the final blow. As Alderman Archie Blain had warned scarcely a decade before, St. Louis's shortsighted leaders had traded "one slum for another slum."

CONCLUSION

After two years of college in Missouri, I moved to New York City to become a fashion designer. I had made all of my clothes for as long as I could remember. I'd studied fashion tailoring for four years at the vocational branch of Vashon High School and earned money sewing for my teachers.

Mama was happy when in 1970 I told her I wanted to move to New York to study apparel design at the Fashion Institute of Technology. She arranged for me to stay with Miss Etta, who was once our boarder in Mill Creek and now lived with her son and his family in the north Bronx. But I think she knew I was following Richie Gershman, a Jewish boy from the Bronx who had somehow found his way to a Presbyterian college in the middle of the cornfields of Tarkio, Missouri. He had a big, curly pseudo-Afro and wore bell-bottom pants he called "dungarees." He played pickup basketball with the black guys on campus and had a thing for black girls (I heard he had a black girlfriend the year before). We fell in love. He wrote to me twice a week from his senior semester abroad in Ireland. He bought me a ring. We planned to marry in New York. That is, until his parents threatened to sit shiva if he married me. He vacillated between honoring his parents' wish and his promise to marry me, until at last I decided his love for me was not strong enough to defy his parents.

I cried, found a job, a place to live, and eventually enrolled in evening classes at FIT.

Upon arriving in New York City, I was distracted from my heartbreak by a new revelation. For as long as I can remember, I had heard the name Pat along with a dozen other names of relatives living in Alabama. Throughout the years, there were pictures of attractive people tucked inside Christmas cards. Except for our cousin Bubba, who visited for a few hours during a layover on his way to California, I had never met any of the Alabama family in person.

In 1957 Gale Patrick Edmunds found his way to Boston after serving two years in the Army. He played trumpet in a jazz band, first in Boston, then in New York City. When I arrived in New York more than a decade later, he was unmarried, a clerk in the US Post Office, and attending art classes in the evening.

We quickly began to peel back the layers of our familial relationship—he was my brother.

We filled in the blank spaces of our separate lives as best we could. Adopted as Aunt Eva's only child, he grew up in a loving family, surrounded by cousins, aunts, uncles, and a grandfather who was an important man in their small town in Alabama. I had grown up in a loving family with my parents and seven sisters and brothers in urban poverty, cut off from most of my mother's extended family.

But Pat and I would have each other in New York, and we became the keepers of Mama's untold story.

My first real job was as a PBX switchboard operator at Kenneth's Salon—hairdresser to some of the rich and famous ladies of New York City's elite. My contacts at the salon led to a few modeling shoots, including one in *Vogue*. But a career as a model was stalled because I wasn't willing to risk the security of a nine-to-five job to pay my rent and tuition. My second job was as a receptionist at the management consulting firm McKinsey & Company. It was the perfect job for getting reading done for my evening classes. Working at McKinsey also coincided with the advent of affirmative action goals and timetables for businesses seeking government contracts. In four years, I was promoted several times, from the front desk receptionist to the support staff recruiter in the human resources department. I read my personnel file with interest when I discovered no one had bothered to remove it when I started working in HR. One interviewer described my appearance as: "Appropriately dressed with a large Afro hairstyle, but not offensive."

Human resources classes at New York University sidelined my design studies at FIT for a while. By the time I finished my degree, I was making too much money to start at the bottom of the fashion industry.

On Friday, July 9, 1976, the country was winding down from a weeklong bicentennial celebration. My phone rang as I was getting dressed for work. It was Honey, who now went by the name "Shep." His greeting was not the usual upbeat "Hey, what's hap'nin' in the Big Apple?" It was solemn and low, followed by a pause. Before I could fill the awkward silence, he said, "Mama died this morning."

The air in my lungs rose to my throat and got stuck there. My chest heaved to make room for a wail that wouldn't come. I could hear his voice through the phone, "Vivian, Vivian, Vivian, are you alright?" When I finally spoke, I asked, "What time did she die?" I wanted to know what I was doing when my mother stopped living. He told me the details he knew. He said when the hospital called, he rushed the few blocks from his nearby apartment. He went directly to her room. They had not yet removed her body. His voice cracked when he said, "I saw her lying there, and I can't get the image out of my mind." I cried with him on the phone. I told him I would get a flight out for St. Louis the next day.

I no longer had a mother. I was consumed by an immediate, childlike feeling of loss and self-pity. I walked around the sunny third-floor apartment on West Ninety-Fifth Street that I shared with my boyfriend, Walter. Mama hadn't gotten a chance to see this apartment. It was a great place, with an exposed brick wall in the living room. I converted the small second bedroom into my sewing room, with a dress mannequin for draping my designs and a sheet of plywood almost as wide as the room as a worktable. I had an opening cut into one end to fit my portable Singer sewing machine. The wood sat atop a pair of two-drawer file cabinets where I stored all my sewing supplies. I trimmed the rough-cut edges of the plywood with duct tape to prevent snags—a custom workspace that Mama would have loved. Moving boxes lined the walls. We would be moving to a larger co-op apartment we'd purchased near Columbia University in a few weeks. Mama wouldn't visit that space either.

The news of her death wasn't entirely unexpected. Mama had been hospitalized a few weeks earlier, and I had taken a long weekend trip to St. Louis to see her. Before my return to New York, she had all her children gather in her hospital room. Only Ferman, who was in the Air Force and stationed in Japan, and Pat were not there. She told us in her usual calm voice that we were "the best part of her life." We all stood with no space between us, staring down at her face that suddenly looked so small. None of us said a word, fearing what she would say next: "I have cancer, and the doctors say I have about three months to live." I remember Tootie gasping and running from the room. Randle followed after her. I don't remember much about what happened next. I'm sure my sisters and I cried—I'm sure she didn't.

Over the next few days, Mama laid out her plans for her remaining days and her funeral. She had it all written down. Mama told us where to find documents and gave us a list of names and numbers of friends and family to call at the appropriate time. She had drafted a short obituary with the exact date left blank. As my sisters and I stood at her bedside, pretending to be as strong as her, she sternly reminded us: "Everything in that house belongs to your Daddy. Do not take anything out without his permission."

We all said, almost in unison, "Yes, ma'am."

Her two final and most emphatic instruction were that she did not want an open casket, and we must not wear black at her funeral. She said with a playful smile, "I want you all to look pretty." I rushed back to New York to arrange for extended time off from my job, and to mock up the obituary so that she could approve it.

She died only nine days after we had all gathered around her hospital bed.

In those days I could jump out of a taxi at LaGuardia Airport, check my bags at the curb, weave through the crowds of passengers going in the opposite direction, and still board the plane with *two* carry-on packages and my purse. I'd taken that Saturday morning flight to St. Louis a half-dozen times over the past five years. This time was different.

I got off the plane at Lambert Field in St. Louis, the two glossy white cardboard hat boxes I had stored in the overhead bin had *Hats by Vivian* printed in an elegant black script on the tops. Inside were six hats I had recently made for an upcoming fashion show at Canaan Baptist Church in Harlem. The ladies in the Pastor's Aid Club sold tickets to the luncheon and would model the hats in the fashion show. I counted on all of them buying at least one of the hats they modeled and ordering another. I did fashion shows for church groups all over Harlem and Brooklyn about once a month. I had a part-time millinery design business I ran out of my apartment after my full-time day job as a recruiter at McKinsey, and classes two evenings a week at FIT.

In the days before heightened airport security, friends and families could crowd around the gate, forming a raucous gauntlet of waving arms, kisses, hugs, and handshakes. Shep stood back from the tangle of greeters as I made my way off the plane. I could barely feel my legs as I dodged and pivoted to reach him. I dropped my hat boxes, we hugged silently, and I could finally cry.

The fashion show in New York was a few weeks off, so I'd have to work double-time to replace the hats I'd brought for my four sisters, my cousin Karen, and me to wear to my mother's funeral.

Daddy, who had not written a check to pay a bill in the past forty years, put on a good face and ran the house with Beverly's help. He moved his elderly mother into the house with him. The two of them were together again, as they had started.

Six months after Mama passed, Daddy took his first airplane trip to New York with my brother Shep for my wedding to Walter Mayo, a handsome Bostonian who had just earned an MBA from Columbia University. Daddy brought with him my mother's silver flatware set as a wedding gift. We had a wonderful few days walking around New York City. He was wide-eyed and laughing with fascination at everything he saw, and happy I had found a "church home" in Harlem. I could tell he was so proud of me. On the morning that he was to return to St. Louis, he stood in my living room in front of our floor-to-ceiling bookshelves and said, "Baby, have you read all those books?" I smiled and said, "Most of them, Daddy."

Truthfully, they were mostly my and Walter's college textbooks and a few dozen classics I had ordered from the Columbia House Book of the Month Club.

When I waved goodbye to Daddy at the gate before he boarded his flight, it was the last time I would see him alive.

He died five months later of a heart attack.

———————

When I was a child, I learned a poem in school—we all did. Written by Bessie A. Stanley, "What Constitutes Success" was published December 11, 1905, in the *Emporia Gazette* of Emporia, Kansas. Many versions of it exist; this is the one I remember.

> He has achieved success who has lived well, laughed often, and loved much; who has gained the respect of his family and friends and the love of little children;
> Who has filled his niche and accomplished his tasks; who has left the world better than he found it; whose life was an inspiration; whose memory is a benediction.

I've thought of this poem over the years, mainly as a personal aspiration. I thought of it again in the context of my parents' lives when I was finishing the concluding manuscript for this book. Writing a book at the age of seventy has given me a surprising new perspective on my parents. I was a mama's girl, and from the beginning, I expected to write a love letter extolling her charm and cleverness. I hope I accomplished that. But through the prism of my own experiences, I began wondering about what her life could have been if she were born forty years later. Would she have given away her firstborn baby ? Would she have compromised her education and relegated her life exclusively to being a wife and mother?

I thought about my father differently as well. He was stern, yes, and sometimes frightening, but he worked and provided for his family as best he could. I'm ashamed to say that I never thought much about his sacrifices until I examined the past and compared it to my own struggles as a parent. What my parents accomplished to keep our family together was nothing short of amazing.

My mother did not live to see me married, to enjoy my children, or to reminisce about the past. I still think about all the secrets and unasked questions. The secrets she had kept from us for so long, I couldn't ask her to share at the end. How could she? What were her deferred dreams? What would she have done differently? I had done what she told me to do: "Move somewhere else so that I can have somewhere to visit." She visited once and was the best houseguest I had ever had. On her last morning in New York, we drank orange spiced tea and ate sweet cornbread with lots of butter. We talked about nothing in particular.

ACKNOWLEDGMENTS

Six months after retirement, I joined a creative writing workshop for "older adults." It seemed like a good fit because the class description said, "For writers of all levels." After several classes, I gathered the confidence to share my writing and steeled myself for feedback. The verbal comments of my fellow writers faded into the fog of self-consciousness, but I've kept all of their written comments. The workshop leader, Kim Lozano, is an award-winning writer and has served as a contributing senior editor at *River Styx Literary Magazine*. She returned my first personal essay with strikethroughs and arrows, inserted and deleted commas, happy faces, and hearts. At the bottom of the last page, she wrote, "Wow! I love this! Keep going." Kim became my cheerleader and coach. She believed I was a writer and pushed me to submit my stories for publication. Kim introduced me to others in the writing community, such as Angela Mitchell. Weeks before the release of her book *Unnatural Habitats,* Angela spent time with me and shared some of her experiences as an author.

I am eternally grateful for family and friends who have loved me and supported every adventure I've been on over the past seventy years. My sister Carol Jean Maben, who paid for my first year of college from her salary and tips as a waitress, has ended most of our phone conversations with, "I love you, and I'm here for you." My brother Shepperd Ross has been my lifelong best friend and promoter. While writing this book, I'd call him almost daily to read what I'd written. If I missed a day, he'd text, "Are you writing?" I couldn't have written much of this book without my other siblings—Thelma (Tootie) McCullum, LaVerne Ross, Randle Ross, and Ferman

Ross—who patiently shared their memories and verified mine throughout my writing process.

Every writer needs early readers, and I rotated through a faithful few. I enjoyed the embrace and enthusiasm of my writers group at St. Louis Oasis. And I'm thankful for my tenth grade English teacher at Vashon High School, Dr. Jacqueline Mitchell (Keaton), who I found on Facebook, fifty years after graduation. I emailed her drafts that she sent back with detailed critiques.

I can't thank my friends Deborah Walker, Jacquie Young, Marilyn Webster Brown, Relda Brooks, Alverta Thomas, Melissa Bode, Bart Holland, Simmie Gellman, and JoAnne Leach enough. They read some of my early drafts riddled with typos that they pretended not to see. My book club members (some for twenty-five years)—Lauren Ming, Alison Nash, Rosalind Johnson, Cheryl Polk, Patricia Burton, Jacqui Turner, Erika Sandiford, Joelle Calhoun, Vanessa Wayne, Donna Black, Lee Haynes, and Sheila Williams—kept my love of books alive and periodically indulged a reading of my latest story during our monthly meetings.

I owe a particular debt of gratitude to David Wright, a talented writer, who for a short time was part of my Oasis writers group. When he announced that he would be taking a break from the group, I asked if he would be willing to continue reading my stories. He agreed, and over the following six months, David read every chapter of my manuscript and gave invaluable feedback. I am in awe of his generosity. I'm also grateful to his wife, Nancy, who was so gracious in allowing me to send early-morning emails to her husband several times a week.

I want to thank Ryan Schuessler, who chose three of my mini-memoir stories for *The St. Louis Anthology* he edited for Belt Publishing. Ryan told his publisher at Belt, Anne Trubek, about my writing, and she suggested that I might have a memoir in my collection of stories. Thank you to Anne for ushering me through the publishing of this book, and Martha Bayne for your creativity, hard work, and amazing editing and marketing skills.

Thanks also to the Missouri History Society Library & Research Center and the St. Louis Room at the St. Louis Public Library, whose staff and researchers provided their expertise.

Finally, to my children, Elizabeth (Lizzie) Mayo and William Ross Gibson, thank you for your support and love. And my dear friend of twenty-plus years, Aubrey Morrison, who makes me happy.